The
GOLDEN
CAGE

The GOLDEN CAGE

Three Brothers, Three Choices, One Destiny

SHIRIN EBADI
Nobel Peace Prize Laureate

Kales Press

Kenneth Kales, Editor and Publisher
Nathaniel Rich, Translator
Lori Lewis, Copy Editor and Proofreader
Jamie Wynne, Editorial Assistant

Cover design by Laura Klynstra
Interior design by Steven Berry

Library of Congress Cataloging-in-Publication Data

'Ibadi, Shirin.
  The golden cage : three brothers, three choices, one destiny / Shirin
Ebadi.
    p. cm.
  ISBN 978-0-9798456-4-2 (alk. paper)
  1. Iran--Politics and government--20th century. 2. 'Ibadi, Shirin. 3.
Women lawyers--Iran--Biography. 4. Lawyers--Iran--Biography. 5.
Nobel Prize winners--Iran--Biography. I. Title.
  DS316.6.I2313 2011
  955.05--dc22
                        2011005921

Contents

If you can't eliminate injustice, at least tell everyone about it.

—ALI SHARIATI

Prologue

"WAIT HERE," I said to my driver. "I'll be back soon."

I checked the rearview mirror to make sure that my hair was still covered by my foulard, but I shouldn't have bothered: in that heat the fabric clung to my forehead. As soon as I stepped out of the car, the Khavaran's torrid desert air hit me like the breath of a furnace. It was the middle of August, and the humidity was unbearable. For a split second I wanted to rush back into the air conditioning. But no, I couldn't, it was silly even to consider it. I adjusted the strap of the handbag on my shoulder and set off at a brisk pace. I passed the old Hindi and Bahá'í tombs and approached the gathering crowd.

For them, this wasn't an unusual sight: a shapeless expanse of grass and dirt, without a fence in sight. The bodies of thousands of political dissidents, crushed beneath the blows of the Pasdaran, had been buried here, one on top of the other, like mowed hay. They'd been denied funerals and interment in Muslim cemeteries. They were *zedd-e enghelab*: counterrevolutionaries. "No memorial services. If you're lucky we'll let you know where you can find the body." That's all that the families of the condemned were told. The dead were discovered after weeks, even months of silence, uncertainty, and absence. That's what had happened to Javad.

I was there for him. Although, for many years, I couldn't figure out why, I had always kept him in my heart. Him and the rest

of our ruined generation, torn apart by half a century of ideo-
logical battles for the soul of my country. Noble Persia; miserable
Iran. On that suffocating day I was there for Javad, from whom
I'd been separated by history. And I was also there for Parì, Abbas,
Alì, and all the others. I was there to make up for the years of
incomprehension and distance, to erase the words of hate and to
recover other words—the words of our old friendships.

I joined a large group of women. They walked slowly, like a
migration, from every direction—mothers, wives, and sisters
holding single carnations or red roses. They all had fiery expres-
sions on their faces and they did not cry. When people die the
way their children did, you can only mourn them at home.

I recognized the woman they called Mother, the spokes-
woman of their grief. She pushed her way into the center of the
crowd. Her sparse white hair was just visible beneath her foulard.
She was about seventy years old. Her son, an engineer who had
studied in America, was buried somewhere in Khavaran.

Mother slowly raised her arm and began to speak. The buzz-
ing stopped.

"Today we're here to remember. We know that blood can't
wash away blood. We are women, not guerrilla fighters. Wives
and mothers and daughters and sisters who have already seen
more than enough violence. Killing the murderers will not bring
back the victims—"

"Silence, infidel! They weren't victims—they were traitors,
zedd-e enghelab—and they deserved to die!"

The voice reverberated in the tense air above our heads. I
looked to see which woman had spoken. She was wrapped, from
head to toe, in a black chador.

We'd been surrounded by women and men of the goruh-e feshar.

The forces that attacked and broke up public demonstrations were once again ready to act.

We pressed together to protect ourselves, shoulder to shoulder, uncertain as to what to do. I remembered what my mother said when I left home: "Shirin *joon*, don't go, it's dangerous." It occurred to me that perhaps, next year, she would be one of those women on the bloody sands of Khavaran, remembering her daughter.

As if obeying a silent order, the *goruh-e feshar* lifted chains and knives into the air. They prepared to attack. Then there was only silence and the dense odor of our fear.

They launched their attack on the outermost circle. The crowd scattered. The women ran off in every direction. The few men among us were immediately seized by the *lebas-shakhsi*—government agents in civilian dress. They beat their backs with clubs, growling, "This should finally put an end to your traitorous demonstrations. Your children don't deserve any memorials. They were enemies of Allah and of Iran. You should have thought about that when you still had time. You should have taught them proper values. It's your fault they're dead!" The *lebas-shakhsi* dragged off their semi-conscious victims, staining the sand with thin streams of blood. Gray-haired women were sprawled all over the ground.

One of the women in chador managed to hit Mother's forehead with a stone. At the sight of the blood, as if driven mad, Mother ran forward even more frantically, despite being buffeted by blows—it was as if all the stones in the desert wouldn't stop her. Some of the others followed her example. Mother was undeterred. The rocks whizzed by her body. "Cowards," she muttered, staring straight ahead.

I couldn't take so much as a single step. I felt paralyzed in front of this surreal display of violence. A woman pushed me aside; I'll never know whether she wanted to help me or if she was only trying to push me out of her way, but that awoke me from my trance. I started to run, following the unknown woman. In a confused haze I saw the faces of weakened women, I heard the metallic sound of chains, smelled the metallic odor of blood. Mother was yelling now—"Cowards!"—but her voice soon faded into the distance.

I tripped over a root, fell, got back up. Any second now I could be swept away or trampled. Or struck down by a scrum in which you couldn't distinguish friends from enemies. My heart leapt into my throat, it echoed in my brain and blotted out every thought. I ran, breathless. A man grabbed me by the arm and I blindly turned to give him a kick.

"Ms. Ebadi? It's me."

It was the driver. He dragged me into the car and we drove away at full speed. Exhausted, I dried the sweat that stung my eyes and tried to calm myself. Feeling cold for the first time, I looked down and realized that in my flight I'd lost my foulard. I lifted one foot onto my knee and saw that the sole was scratched and bleeding. I watched a thick drop of blood fall on the floor mat, and only then did I feel the burning sensation of my wounds.

Old Friendships

THE FIRST THING I REMEMBER is the scent of the tea, which sat on top of a stove that I wasn't tall enough to reach. Then I remember the water boiling in the potbellied teapot, and Simin's quick hands, selecting the smallest pot from the cabinet above my head.

"Shirin *joon*, move over, you're going to make me drop something."

Other hands nudged me away while Simin opened the box of tea—she only used the tips, the best part of the plant. A few teaspoons, then the boiling water. I watched, fascinated, as the fragrant smoke escaped into the air. Simin placed the small pot delicately on top of the larger one, which was still half-filled with water. Beneath, the low flame.

"You shouldn't let it boil," Parì, always didactic, told me every time.

And Simin's hands, Parì's voice, the scent of the tea, and the milky white kitchen walls closed around me to form the warm cocoon of a childhood memory.

I grew up with Parì and her brothers. Our mothers had been best friends since they were five or six years old. At the time they had both been living in Hamadan, a city in northwest Iran that had once been, under the name Ecbatana, the country's capital. It was a childhood friendship, born from a handful of almond cookies, but it had managed to endure the turbulent years of childhood, a restless adolescence, two marriages, and two moves. On top of that Simin was married at a very young age to Hossein, a *bazari* from Tehran—but through everything they stayed in touch. Letters traveled across long distances with the regularity of a personal diary, disclosing shared secrets, recipes, and memories. And in 1948 when my mother, now married with children, moved to the capital, the friendship between the women, as often is the case, created a tight bond between their families.

My father, Mohammad Alì, was relaxed in the company of Hossein, who was always joking and quick to smile. They subscribed to opposing life philosophies: my father was a demanding and combative man, a jurist by profession, with a loyal and serious manner that some people mistook for coldness, but the truth was that he simply had a passion for justice. He had raised each of his four children—one boy and three girls—as equals, because he believed that equal education and respect for others should begin with the family. He had strong ideals that he followed strictly and had inculcated in all of us, convinced that no one should be exempt from participating in the civic and political life of the country. No matter the cost.

Hossein, despite being an honest and righteous man, had a more conciliatory attitude. He had inherited his father's carpet business, which was based in the heart of the town bazaar, and he ran it with his younger brother, Nader. The business did well enough to provide both of them with a respectable salary, though it would never make them rich. If they had been only slightly more enterprising, they might have been able to follow other Iranian shopkeepers into export trade at a fortuitous moment— demand for exotic objects in Europe and America was extremely high at the time. But Hossein loved his life and considered his free time sacred. Like my father, he sought to avoid creating differences between his children, both in their education and in the way they prepared for life as adults. He hoped, of course, that the boys would succeed him in the management of the bazaar, and he was certain that Parì would get married and have children. He tried to teach them about tolerance. He had known too many people and heard too many bad stories; above all he could not accept the sin of an impoverished mind.

His true passion was to be in the presence of other people, and one that he brought home with him. He was proud of his hospitality and easily made friends with every type of person, inviting them to dinner, always happy to hear new stories. It was like traveling for him—breathing the air of distant countries that he'd never visited. Simin encouraged him in this. She always cooked too much, even when she wasn't expecting guests, knowing that her husband was likely to show up with someone who might do honor to her meals.

Despite their differences, my father and Hossein formed a quiet friendship. In our long evenings at the home of the *bazari*, they loved to sit after dinner on the low embroidered cushions under the corner window. The wives stayed in the kitchen and the children were strictly forbidden from disturbing their fathers' conversation, which ranged from the personal to the philosophical. They spoke of politics, inflation, wholesale prices, and business law, about which my father was an expert. But looking back now I realize that this conversation was simply a preliminary phase, a kind of warming-up exercise to prolong the anticipation—and thus the pleasure—of their favorite pastime: *takteh-nard, a* variation of backgammon. After their small talk had subsided, Hossein would pull out a gorgeous wooden box that had been designed for the game of *takteh-nard*. His father had acquired it when he was a young novice merchant. It had a chessboard design on the outside, and on the inside notches had been carved into the wood to hold the natural colored and dark painted pieces. Hossein moved a small card table, which normally leaned against the wall, between them. He opened the box with great ceremony, unhinging the mechanism in the middle of the lid. The case opened into two halves, the finely-carved pieces sparkling like jewels against the velvet lining. These opening rites always elicited the same exclamation from my father: "It's not often you see such beautiful objects!"

Only then would they immerse themselves in an interminable sequence of games. For hours you could hear the clink of the dice and the wood-on-wood sound of the pieces as they were deftly moved around the board. And the playful taunting of the men trying to demoralize each other.

"If you need more time to ponder your move, I can go make another cup of tea," my father would say, the moment Hossein's hand hesitated above a piece.

"Sounds like you're looking for an excuse to quit, since you clearly have no chance of winning," Hossein retorted.

I still remember, after all these years, those routine barbs, so typical of their style of play and the strength of their friendship. And I mourn the time when those amusing banterings were the only quarrels that could be heard between the walls of their happy home.

THE MARRIAGE OF HOSSEIN AND SIMIN was soon blessed by the arrival of a son, Abbas. From the beginning he was vigorous and healthy: at his birth he weighed more than four kilograms, he'd kick and scream for hours, crying twice as loud as all the other babies, and—most unusual for a newborn—he had a full head of thick, dark hair. His swarthiness became more pronounced as a young man: to go along with his hair, he grew a beard that left a bluish shadow on his olive skin, and would grow tangled if left unshaven for just a few days. He was tall, strong—imposing even—with a face that, perhaps because it was so dark, always seemed to be composed in a serious expression. Hossein regarded him with pride; he worshipped his firstborn son. Abbas recipro-cated his affection, trying hard to take after his father. He had inherited his father's sense of integrity and his profound love of family, but not his joviality or sense of humor. I remember that on the few occasions in which a smile appeared, somewhat reluc-tantly, on his face—the rigid features softening unexpectedly—he seemed like a different person.

Abbas never showed particular interest in having brothers and sisters to look after and instruct. It took the family seven years of miscarriages and holy pilgrimages before the arrival of their first daughter, Parì, who would become one of my best friends. Then, in 1950, came the much-anticipated second son, Javad, who my mother always said was the most beautiful baby she'd ever seen. The most stubborn, too, added Simin. She carried Javad in her womb two weeks past his due date, and he seemed like he didn't ever want to come out. But when the moment finally arrived, he won her over with his two full, pink cheeks—and the light tuft of down on his brow.

Restless and independent from infancy, Javad was consumed by a voracious curiosity and was incapable of playing with other children, whose games bored him. At just four years old, when

Hossein sat down in his armchair to read the newspaper, Javad would perch on his shoulders and listen to the hymnal rhythm of his father mouthing the words of the articles. He figured out almost immediately the hidden mechanism behind the letters' sinuous designs and within a few years he was reciting the words for his father well before Hossein had time to read them himself.

In his eagerness to grow up, Javad spurned the company of children his own age; he tried, instead, to fit in with the adults. Hossein's attempts to keep him in line were completely futile, especially when guests were over; he followed along with their conversations and didn't hesitate to ask questions when he didn't understand something. Simin scolded him, but deep down she was proud of her intelligent and ever more handsome son— Javad, with his golden complexion, his ruffled curls, and the large, intense eyes of an ancient Persian warrior, was the envy of all the other mothers. His most winning quality, however, was his smile, which revealed perfect white teeth, illuminating, like a lamp, his delicate features. Javad was aware of his appeal and learned early on how to use his smile to obtain what he wanted—from his parents, of course, but also from Parì and from me and my sisters. He even had the nerve to insinuate himself into his father's *takteh-nard* games. At first he silently crouched at the edge of the card table, closely observing the action; soon he became bold enough to comment on the players' moves with a quiet whistle that he tried to disguise by coughing. When he finally asked my father for "the honor" of challenging him to a match, my father, rather amused, accepted, and proceeded to rout him in four minutes— though he did feel a little guilty when he saw the disappointed look on the boy's face. Javad did not give up, and soon begged for a rematch; he was defeated again, but he returned to the fray at every possible opportunity, since for my father even this "lesser" challenge, waged on the sideline of his battles against his old friend Hossein, had quickly become habit. My father did restrain, however, from taunting him, since it would have been unkind to provoke a little boy.

One night Parì and I were in her room talking about such a momentous subject as the new Parisian fashions when we were interrupted by a shout from the living room. We ran in and found Javad all aglow, standing beside the *takteh-nard* table. One glance at the placement of the pieces, and my father's smile, and I understood: the boy had won.

On the way home I still couldn't believe it. "Javad was so happy," I said to my father. "It was generous of you to let him win."

My father cast me a sidelong glance and, after a moment of hesitation, said, "Shirin *joon*, I didn't let him win." Then he added, in a voice that seemed directed more to himself than to us, "That boy's going to go places. . . . If he's able to reign in that rebellious nature of his, and if there's any justice in the world—he'll go places."

Many years later I recalled that hot, distant night when Javad first experienced the thrill of combining luck and strategy to achieve victory. He didn't realize back then that the challenges he'd face later in life would not be so easily overcome.

2

The House in Abbas Abad

PARÌ AND HER FAMILY lived in the newly developed residential neighborhood of Abbas Abad. The free-standing white house, with its large garden and simple, sturdy structure, cost Hossein twenty years of savings and sacrifice—a fact he made sure to point out to the many guests who complimented him on the elegance of his home. The back of the house opened up to a beautiful portico where our parents sat in the summer evenings, gazing out at the profile of the Alborz mountain range. At the base of the portico columns Simin planted jasmine that flowered from April to August; when the plant lost its white flowers, it meant it was time to abandon the large outside table and dust off the *korsì*, the traditional dining table with a heater beneath it, for use inside during the winter.

The house was surrounded by a high wall to ensure the family's privacy. A wrought-iron gate guarded the entrance. The thick metal lattice may have blocked prying glances, but it also made it the most imposing entranceway in the city. "Have you ever seen anything so ugly?" Parì cried, inserting the heavy key into the lock.

But behind the bizarre whorls lay hidden a small corner of paradise: The gate opened up to a gurgling fountain, in which Simin scattered bread crumbs to attract sparrows and doves. On either side there extended a wide lawn where Parì, our brothers, and I would run about for hours, and then collapse, exhausted, in the shadow of young lime trees. In one corner, right at the foot of the Alborz range, was Simin's marvelous rose garden, which in the hot summer months filled the air with its perfume.

I was overjoyed as soon as I saw the wide, tree-lined avenues of Abbas Abad: I knew that I would soon be greeted warmly by Simin, who was always happy to see her best friend's children. During the pleasant time of year, the house bustled with relatives, friends, acquaintances, and Hossein's clients, who stopped by to enjoy the coolness of the garden and the cooking of Simin, whose glorious cuisine was acclaimed throughout Tehran. Her table was always crowded with large trays filled with rice mixed with fava beans and other vegetables, accompanied by various meat dishes. In bowls of yogurt there soaked little leaves of mint or bits of cucumber, to which the children added raisins. *Kuku* was removed from the oven to cool in terra cotta containers; I looked forward to the soft confection of spinach, egg, and black current that lay beneath its thin golden crust. Simin refused to tell anyone—even my mother—how she'd made its crispy texture; she said she had learned it from the wife of an Armenian merchant who had sworn her to absolute secrecy. As we offered her praise she demurred that the lamb in the *khoresht fesenjun* wasn't properly cooked or that the halva, sizzling with butter, lacked sufficient sugar, or had too much saffron. But her halva was in fact the best, and often Parì and I crept into the kitchen to sneak some sweets from the tray that had already been prepared for the table.

After the large spring and summer parties, there followed the quiet monotony of the winter nights: my father and Hossein isolated themselves in their little corner, while my mother and Simin warmed their feet, covered by quilts under the *korsi*. They chatted for hours, sipping tea and listening to the radio. My brother, my sisters, and I, too restless to sit under the heavy blankets, escaped by playing with Pari and Javad. Abbas rarely joined us, since we were too young for him; he preferred to be on his own, neither an adult nor a child, lazily turning the pages of a book, glancing over at us every so often.

He was, in a way, an older brother to all of us, but he watched over Javad with an acute attention—a necessity given Javad's impulsive tendency to get into trouble in the most unlikely ways. I remember a particularly muggy July afternoon when our parents instructed us to stay on the top floor, while they talked downstairs in the darkened living room. It was too hot to sleep and Javad, furious at being excluded from the adults' conversations, kept tossing and turning in bed. There was a rustle of the sheets and then I saw him slide out the window.

"Where are you going?" I whispered.

"I'm hungry. I'm going to get some cherries."

"But your father said you can't—they're too high up."

"No one will find out. You coming or not?"

I didn't say anything, torn between the fear of getting into trouble and the temptation of those sweet, juicy cherries. Javad interpreted my silence as a refusal and, without waiting for me, climbed up on the windowsill. The branches of one of the smaller lime trees just reached our window; with a short jump Javad was free. Proud of myself for not following him, but somewhat worried, too, I went over to the window to keep an eye on him. After all, I was the older child and felt responsible. I watched him climb down the lime tree with great agility, while he also looked around to make sure no one was following. If his father caught him, there'd be trouble. He ran to the base of the high wall and, using another tree, jumped on top of it. He was as quick, stealthy, and nimble as a cat. It was clearly not the first time he'd done this.

In the neighboring garden, right at the top of the wall, were the branches of a cherry tree. Javad began to pick the fruit, dropping them into his mouth. Every so often he would turn to glance back at his house. He was perfectly visible, but by now he felt safe, even triumphant in his mission. Seeing me in the window, he waved and made a silly face. He looked so ridiculous that I burst into laughter.

"Shirin? What are you doing over there?"

I turned around with a start. Abbas was standing in the doorway.

"Where's Javad?" He glanced at me and then the empty bed. Before I could answer he was beside me at the window.

"Oh no. No way."

Everything happened very quickly after that. Abbas ran into the living room to tell his parents what was going on. They rushed upstairs, followed by my parents.

"Javad, get down from there!" yelled Hossein. "Javad, do you hear me? I said get down immediately. We're going to have a little talk, you and me."

But Javad showed no sign of moving. The threat of punishment unnerved him. His golden smile had collapsed into a simper that made him look like he were on the edge of tears.

"Javad, come down!"

"I . . . I can't," he said, and then burst into sobs.

Abbas appeared from behind the house, holding a ladder. He leaned it against the wall and began to climb up.

"Don't get excited, Javad, it's all right. I'll take care of this." His assuredness calmed Javad. "Want to climb up on my shoulders? Good, just like that, you're almost there. Right—way to go. Now hold on tight."

Abbas climbed down with his little brother on his shoulders. Hossein ran over and hugged Javad. Then he let go and slapped him loudly, twice, in front of everyone.

After that experience Javad developed an aversion to cherries, since they reminded him of the most embarrassing moment of his childhood, but he did learn to rely on the silent and reassuring presence of Abbas who, from that moment on, was his hero.

THE DIFFERENCES THAT both divided and brought together our fathers were the same that tied me to Parì. I was attracted to her easy-going, cheerful manner: like Javad she was curious and enterprising, but she also had a seriousness about her, which had been instilled by her role as older sister and by the responsibility, which she shared with her mother, of managing the house. But more than Simin she resembled Hossein, having the same sense of humor and the ability to see the absurdity in any situation. Since she was two years older than me, she quickly became my guide to things that remained unknown to me. While I was amusing myself with my coloring books, she taught me how to play with dolls; while I was discovering the first secrets of femininity, she invited me into the kitchen to try her mother's recipes.

At that time cooking was always a pleasure, almost a game, and we loved to do it together. We prepared *ghorme sabzi* and sweets like *falude.* But the *chelow kebab* was far and away our favorite dish, as it is for most Iranians. It's made with a plate of rice—but finer than the kind you normally find in the West—accompanied by lean meat of the highest quality. It's generally served on a tray, preferably one made of porcelain, with a pinch of saffron. The meat is cut in small, thin pieces, then grilled. You can serve it with butter, egg yolks, sumac, and dried fruit. But Parì didn't agree about the dried fruit.

"It's a funny taste," she said. "I don't know, I wouldn't use it."

"OK, Parì, whatever you say," I relented. Then I added, under my voice, "I don't mind it though."

She was always dragging me to the American films that screened in the Tehran cinemas and she kept me updated on the latest in Western couture, for which she harbored an intense passion. In the thirties Reza Shah, who had recently been installed on the Peacock Throne by a coup d'état, had tried to bring about a rapid modernization of the country, in an effort to mimic the West. He encouraged the adoption of European dress: Soon the men were directed to wear jackets and pants, and the women were prohibited from wearing the *hijab*, the traditional Islamic veil. Whoever didn't want to show her hair could, at most, wear a hat; the police were authorized to stop anyone who dared to wear traditional dress and forcefully tear off their chadors in the middle of the street. For months—even years, in some cases—the more conservative families ordered their mothers and daughters not to leave their property lest they suffer the shame of being seen in public with their heads bared.

The prohibition of the veils was abolished when the new shah came to power, eager as he was to ingratiate himself amongst the members of the clergy. In the fifties and sixties, the country had stabilized and European fashion was all the rage for girls of our generation, especially those in the cities. Parì, who liked to think of herself as avant-garde, ordered subscriptions to French and

English magazines and asked the family seamstress to make her clothing modeled after the latest fashions. Despite not sharing her full enthusiasm for the West, I always ran to Parì for advice on questions of style and for the latest news about her love affair with Europe.

Whenever I was in a bad mood, a phone call from her was all it took to cheer me up. Parì could always see the good in things, while I constantly tormented myself with anxieties. She would try to distract me and lighten my mood. When I think back now to the things that used to bother me—a school election, an argument with my parents—I realize how right she was. I wasn't thinking straight back then. But before long, "not thinking" would become impossible.

"You think too much, Shirin *joon*," she told me. "This is your problem. Don't think, just try to have fun." "And how do I not think?" I asked skeptically.

"I don't know," was her response. "But too many thoughts ruin the skin!" and laughing, she passed her hand over my face, as if to erase my imaginary wrinkles.

3
Mossadegh's Pen

ON MAY 28, 1901, Mozaffar ad-Din Shah signed a contract
that granted an Englishman, William Knox D'Arcy, the rights to
nearly every oil field in Iran for the next sixty years. In return the
shah would receive 16 percent of the profits. In 1914 D'Arcy sold
his stake to the British government, which immediately sought to
maneuver itself into Iranian politics.

To protect its economic interests in the nation, England
needed a strong ally and military support. To this end, in 1921,
it supported a coup d'état brought by an unassuming Cossack
colonel, Reza Khan, forcing Ahmad Shah to nominate him for
the office of prime minister. While the shah was satisfying his
desire for world travel and increasingly distanced himself from
Iran, Reza Khan, with the support of the Parliament—the Majlis—nominated himself for head of state, and declared the end
of the Qajar dynasty. On April 25, 1926, Reza Khan ascended to
the Peacock Throne under the name of Reza Shah Pahlavi; this
surname, which he had adopted in accordance with European
custom, meant "of the Parthian language."

After consolidating his supporters, Reza Shah became increasingly hostile in his dealings with the British government until, in
1932, he declared that their oil contract had been annulled. In
response, the English built up their military presence in the Persian Gulf and threatened to confiscate the shah's foreign bank

accounts, but they were ultimately forced to draft a new pact. The amount of oil profits reserved for Iran was increased to 20 percent.

Though their differences with Great Britain had been partially resolved, a new and far more serious point of conflict was emerging on the world's political stage due to Adolf Hitler. Reza Shah, enchanted with Hitler's ideas and his apparently unstoppable political ascent, reached out to German diplomats, but his ovations were ignored. At the outbreak of the Second World War the Iranian government officially declared its neutrality, announcing that it would not allow any foreign forces to cross its borders. The choice of neutrality constituted a form of indirect support for Hitler, because it prevented the Allies from passing through Iran to reinforce the Soviet front, which was being besieged by the Nazis.

In July 1941 the Allies asked the Iranian government for the final time to expel all of its German citizens and allow supplies to be shipped to the Russian military. Reza Shah, trying to stall for time, reaffirmed Iran's neutrality. After every diplomatic option had failed, the Allies invaded the country and forced the shah to abdicate in favor of his son, Mohammad Reza Pahlavi.

The new shah took power in 1941 and immediately adopted a more open attitude. At least until 1949, when, after being lightly wounded in an assassination attempt, he gradually returned to the methods of his father: despotic rule and restrictions of political and civil liberties. It was hardly the last disillusionment for the Iranian people, who for so long have waited for a true liberator.

If Reza Shah's star was in decline—he didn't even manage to procreate an heir to the throne—Mohammad Mossadegh's shined brightly. A long-time parliamentary member of the National

Front, he was also president of the Majlis's Oil Commission, and succeeded where Reza Shah had failed. In March 1951 he passed a law to nationalize the oil industry, revoking the pact made with England. The British government appealed to the International Court of Justice in The Hague and then to the United Nations' Security Council. After Mossadegh appeared in person to defend the rights of the Iranian people, he obtained a favorable ruling that terminated the oil pact.

In his homeland he was welcomed back as a national hero, and received honors from all over the world. Elderly and in ill-health, he was accustomed to receiving guests and diplomats in his bedroom, the shah included, maintaining that combination of deference and pride so typical of the Iranian character. An elite Swiss education had tempered his eastern roots, shaping him into a leader who was both aristocratic and populist, modern and traditional. According to some historians, it was his example that also inspired Gamal Abdul Nassar to reclaim for Egypt the rights to the Suez Canal and to seek liberation from English interference.

Reza Shah did not look favorably upon Mossadegh's rapid ascension, but he was forced to nominate him for prime minister, and watched powerlessly as his initiatives dismantled centuries of absolute rule. Mossadegh profited from the large support of those who hoped to restrict royal privileges and move Iran toward a constitutional monarchy. During his reign, the shah had only nominal power and the country was governed for the first time by regularly elected representatives. Some changes, however, like the agrarian and fiscal reforms, threatened religious groups and members of the upper class, who feared that the government was flirting too heavily with communism.

Over time, the shah found ways to bring about destruction of
the exceptionally popular Mossadegh. He allied himself with the
American and English secret services and, in an effort to ruin the
prime minister plenipotentiary, he signed off on the infamous
Operation Ajax, which had been devised by Kermit Roosevelt Jr.,
the nephew of President Theodore Roosevelt. On August 16, 1953,
Mohammad Reza Shah dismissed Mossadegh, who protested,
denouncing the attempted coup d'état in the press. Crowds of
antimonarchists, liberals, and students took to the streets to support the prime minister and to demand the proclamation of the
Republic. In a determined escalation of violence that claimed the
lives of thousands of young people, the military crushed the protestors and arrested Mossadegh.

THE DAY OF THE PRIME MINISTER'S ARREST, Simin, distraught,
called all the neighbors.

"Have you seen Abbas?"

We were in Hamadan, at our grandmother's house; our parents had sent us out of Tehran so we'd be far away from the violence in the city. If Abbas had shown up at our house, he would
have found it locked. Simin only told us much later about that
afternoon, spent searching in anguish for her son after he hadn't
returned from school. He hadn't been to the shop, or to the house.
She stayed on the telephone, sobbing, while her husband Hossein ran through the streets, trying to avoid getting trapped in
the protests. In those days, the radio stations, which had recently
been taken over by the shah, continued to celebrate the end of
the prime minister's rule and the liberation of the people. But
in actuality, the second you left your house you'd see corpses in

the streets and protesters clashing with police. When Mossadegh rejected his dismissal, his supporters had hoped that he might be reinstated and they gathered in the public squares chanting his name. The military shot at the protestors, including those who were students. They even shot at children.

For Abbas's parents, that afternoon lasted an eternity. For their oldest son however, it passed in an instant and it was destined to seal his fate. His parents didn't know it, but their son's life had begun to change. For many months, his young and impressionable mind had already been molded by speeches made by the shah's supporters.

The neighborhood where they lived, Abbas Abad, was constructed in the early fifties by order of the shah, and it was inhabited mostly by state officials. Abbas often visited the other children and their families, and he developed a fascination with the glory of the military ethos, which resonated with his own innate sense of duty. Long conversations with his friends and comments made by their parents had transformed the shah into a hero in his eyes—the one and only protector of Iran's grandeur and integrity. He had even hung in his room the portrait of Mohammad Reza and his beautiful queen, Soraya. And for months he had listened to the speeches of his friends' fathers, almost all of them officials who had lost faith in Mossadegh.

"You'd have thought the nationalization of the oil industry would have resolved everything," they complained. "But it's only made inflation rise." The crisis following the embargo by England's protest to the nationalization had, among other things, also forced heavy cuts in the military budget.

"And without the specialized English personnel, when will the refineries be able to function again at full capacity?" they added, imagining a future of needless sacrifice. They also worried that their traditional values might erode amidst an onslaught of accelerated reforms. Iran had been a major power for centuries, drawing its strength from its nobility and its traditions. Too many changes in too short a time risked weakening, and even destabilizing, the society.

"Mossadegh was wrong. He's bringing Iran to its knees, just so he can hand it over to his communist buddies," the officials darkly concluded.

Abbas absorbed these ideas in silence at first, but started to get upset when he heard about Mossadegh's abuses of power and the suffering of his beloved shah. At home he reported the things he'd learned, but every political discussion withered under Hossein's placid and disinterested gaze. Abbas's newfound political fervor didn't bother him, convinced as he was that his son would soon overcome this infatuation and go back to being the calm, serious person he'd always been; besides, it wasn't long now before he'd begin working in the shop alongside his father. However, when the soldiers besieged the Majlis, the radio networks, and all the media companies, Hossein feared the mob might have dragged Abbas into some debate, brawl, or worse. It wasn't like him to be so late.

But Abbas wasn't himself anymore. For the first time he had cast off his impeccable sense of responsibility and composure, inflamed by a higher duty: to defend his king. Alternating between running and hitching rides on the back of the vans that passed by, Abbas followed the procession of soldiers without attracting notice. In the confusion he snuck past the perimeter walls and into the prime minister's palace.

I remember how his black eyes sparkled when, several days later, for the last time, he told me and his sister about his adventure:

"We arrested Mossadegh! I mean, the military arrested him, but I was right there with them. You should've seen him, Mossadegh, when they dragged him out: he looked like a scared old man. And his ministers, hiding like mice from their neighbors! I feel embarrassed for them."

When he finally returned home that afternoon, disheveled and hot from his day, his parents couldn't bring it upon themselves to reprimand him. There was no point: he was lost in a new world and it'd be impossible to pull him out of it. He held out a pen, grimy with dust and sweat. It was Mossadegh's pen. Abbas was so happy that he didn't even notice the tears in Simin's eyes. That morning she had watched her eldest son leave her house; in the evening he had returned a soldier.

The news of the arrest spread quickly. It had been a rapid, simple operation. The military had surrounded Mossadegh's palace and attacked his last loyal supporters. Bullets had rained down on them for three hours, leaving nothing but plaster and ruins, before the resistance finally surrendered. It was said that more than three hundred people died. Forty or perhaps fifty soldiers, selected from the most loyal battalions, raided the palace of the ex-prime minister. They came out a little while later, dragging behind them the seventy-one-year-old man who had been marked as Iran's number one enemy. A crowd gathered around them, happy to observe the fall of the man who, until the previous day, had controlled the country's destiny.

As soon as the soldiers carried off the prisoner, a large, enraged crowd gathered around the palace and surrounding buildings. Soldiers and citizens, transformed into common rabble by the fury of the historic occasion, trampled the floor in rage, pulling out the rugs, kicking the furniture, and grabbing anything they could get their hands on. "Thank God!" they yelled. "Long live the shah, long live Iran!" as if they could avenge, in a single day, the economic difficulties and uncertainty of the last years.

If you ignored the indignation against the English engineers, and ignored the ambiguous signals sent by the American politicians, Mossadegh was the one traitor who could be taken down. He was a weak link who would've easily been overthrown by the communists—and once that happened, the shah would be ruined. It would've all been over then. That, at least, was what Abbas repeated to us in the weeks that followed—the dangers of communism and the necessity of forming an alliance with the United States. But Abbas was one of those people who had run through the palace during the assault. He had followed the group of looters and zigzagged haphazardly, pushed and pulled by the excesses of the crowd. He still didn't fully understand the source of the violent hatred he had witnessed, but he felt like he had become a protagonist in an important historical moment and figured that, in his own little way, he had done something valuable for his nation. Abbas—unlike those who were too naïve, unlike even his parents—had perceived in time the danger they faced and had rallied behind a just cause. That day he had taken from Mossadegh's desk a fountain pen, black with gold trim, a reminder of the punishment the shah's forces had inflicted upon the traitor.

Hossein and Simin should have punished their oldest son for having frightened them in this way. But they certainly couldn't have done anything to undo the impression that the arrest had made on Abbas. He loved the story about the pen and repeated it to everyone who came by the house, and to us, whenever we would humor him, which was less and less often. From that moment on, whenever he wanted to make a solemn oath, he would swear "on His Majesty's crown."

My father didn't tolerate this kind of talk because he'd been forced out of his job for being a fervent supporter of Mossadegh. He sat around the house all day, silent, his children uncertain of the magnitude of what had happened. Like many Iranians he had concluded that politics was a dirty game, in which we, the people, had no role. On that day in 1953, he banned political conversations in our house and made us become—as much as was possible—ignorant of everything related to politics.

When the former prime minister Mossadegh was put on trial for high treason, he bravely defied the shah's ire, displaying for the last time the oratorical ability that, not long ago, had helped him wrest control of the oil industry from the British. He was condemned to three years of solitary confinement in prison, followed by house arrest until his death, which came in 1967. General Zahedi was nominated in his place, a man notorious for being a Nazi sympathizer during the Second World War.

The shah, who had withdrawn to a giant suite at the Hotel Excelsior in Rome during the period of greatest danger, now returned to Iran to assist in the trial and celebrate his return to power. He personally thanked the man responsible for Operation Ajax, Kermit Roosevelt Jr., saying to him, "I owe the throne to Allah, to the people, to the military, and to you." With these words he undid centuries of proud Iranian independence, implicitly recognizing Iran's subjugation—though it was never an official colony—to the United States. The military arrested members of the opposition, or at least those they presumed to be members of the opposition, imprisoning thousands of young people.

In exchange for its support, the United States obtained favorable contracts for American oil companies, installing loyalists in cabinet positions and restocking the country with an enormous quantity of arms, transforming Iran into their own puppet military force in the Middle East.

During Bill Clinton's presidency, Secretary of State Madeline Albright gave a speech declaring that the coup orchestrated by the CIA in Iran was a horrible blunder, and she asked the Iranian people for forgiveness. Many historians argue that if Mossadegh had remained in power, his reforms would have forestalled the radicalization of the shah's regime and, as a result, prevented the Islamic Revolution.

4
One Soldier's Destiny

ON THE DAY OF MOSSADEGH'S ARREST Abbas decided to enter the military academy. Hossein—though he had made a strong effort to educate his children about free will, encouraging them to pursue their own path in life—tried to dissuade him. Not only because he'd always hoped to hand his business over to his son, but because he saw that his family was being swallowed by hatred, ideology, and division. His son, however, was not to be deterred.

"They've brainwashed him—can't you see?" he asked his wife, losing his temper. "Since when has a member of our family joined the military? We've always been merchants, all the way down the line."

Simin was in agreement. Like any mother, the idea that her son might be a soldier scared her. But she knew that her firstborn, once he got started on something, would follow it through to the end and be impervious to any interference. She tried to reassure her husband with the observation that, given the state of the economy, the academy was one of the most practical options for employment.

"In the army he'll have a secure job and a regular salary."

"I can give him a job and a salary myself, if that's all he's looking for."

"There's no point in getting worked up. If you can't change your fate, you have to change your attitude."

Simin ultimately supported her oldest son by keeping him at a distance—not from her home so much as from the neighbors' houses. In recent months she had often walked in on Abbas staring out his window to the courtyard next door—the same one where, years earlier, Javad had stolen the fruit. Colonel Ahmad lived there with his wife and their ten children. The youngest had just begun to talk but Abbas had become inseparable from the oldest son, Farzam. It was thanks to Farzam more than anyone else that Abbas had begun to visit that family, passing hours listening to the colonel's rambling disquisitions on the shah. But the house did hold another attraction: Touran, Farzam's twin sister.

Abbas had never spoken with her, though he had encountered her often as she slipped silently through the halls or helped her mother serve tea. She moved in a light, graceful manner, as if she were dancing, and her clothes barely rustled, clinging delicately to her supple figure. Her voice enchanted him: low and velvety, without high tones, and tenderly affectionate with her younger siblings. Abbas admired her long tapering fingers cradling the teacups and he imagined holding her hand in his. The thought alone was enough to make him tremble with desire. He was so taken by Touran that he didn't notice the way she flushed whenever he came over.

He began to spy on her from his window. He felt guilty because he knew he was violating the family's privacy, but that didn't stop him from doing it any less. He watched her watering the geraniums, collecting sprigs of jasmine to put in the linen drawers, playing with the children and rolling with them in the grass. Touran had noticed Abbas's interest and his maneuvering, and she behaved even more charming as a result, but she pretended not to notice his discreet courtship; she knew that if he suspected he'd been discovered, he wouldn't dare show his face again.

The first time that Abbas finally got the courage to meet eyes with the girl, he knew he was in love.

Simin was not without sympathy for the two of them. She liked the girl: serious, educated, well raised, and she loved children. But the family worried her: Colonel Ahmad was a monarchist convinced that he was a member of the shah's inner circle, Farzam was already enrolled at the military academy, and who knew how many of his brothers would also undertake a military career. She dreamt of a different future for Abbas: an honest, tranquil job far removed from politics. She had seen the nation's flag change too many times already. The power of Mohammad Reza, who pompously proclaimed himself the *Shhanshh*, the King of Kings, was as fragile as that of his father, a semiliterate soldier who had been elevated to the throne almost by chance and was quickly ruined by scheming allies. The same class of people were now influencing her son.

But Simin reasoned with her heart and had no way of imagining how history would still progress. Instability, unfortunately, is far too predictable in a country like Iran, where more than 50 percent of the national revenue comes from oil. For ages Russia, the United Kingdom, and then the United States competed for Iran's immense resources, ruining alliances and dynasties whenever it benefited them. As a result the regime always remained at the mercy of foreign, oversized interests: the taxes paid by the citizens never constituted a significant proportion of the national budget, which received its riches from the oilfields and therefore had little accountability to popular consensus. Democracy exists when the people control the state: When that happens the government is forced to respect and listen to their people. But in Iran, how could the people have any power if they depended on the state for their wealth?

DESPITE HIS FATHER'S OPPOSITION and his mother's concerns, Abbas enrolled in the military academy. During his rare visits home, he returned to his window and waited for Touran to appear so that he could reassure himself that she hadn't gotten engaged in his absence. When he finished his official course instruction, he earned the sympathy of a general who had appreciated his integrity and his patriotic spirit, and this general helped to pave the way for a brilliant career. Abbas loved his work and believed in it. He looked proudly upon the motto that was scrawled on the walls of every army barrack in the country: "For God, For Shah, For Country." It was a slogan that praised the three pillars of Iranian society: faith first, then the king, whose authority rested on his role as defender of the Shiite religion, and finally the nation, which existed thanks to his protection. As a famous mullah once said, even the bees have a queen, because a society can't exist without a ruler. Abbas firmly believed this.

Wearing his new, freshly-ironed uniform, he felt as if he finally had something to offer to Touran. When they passed on the street, he found the courage to smile at her. He didn't know it but she had been waiting for that moment, too. As soon as she returned his smile, Abbas was overwhelmed by happiness.

They married shortly after and moved into a delightful two-story cottage with a large garden, not far from their families. When they were expecting their first child, Abbas swore on His Majesty's crown that he'd be the best father in the world, and prayed for a son. In the following months he managed to remodel the house and even construct a cradle for the baby. He wanted his firstborn to feel welcome.

One night, when Touran was in her seventh month, she awoke to piercing cramps. She screamed in pain. Abbas ran for the midwife, called his mother and mother-in-law, and then waited in the next room, going over in his mind the preparations for the little party they were going to have for his child. Sour black cherry syrup, apple and pistachio tarts—and he'd invite his soldiers-in-arms and even his old school friends. Anything for his firstborn.

Abbas had organized everything, had fretted over every tiny detail, and was prepared to accept a son into his life. But he wasn't prepared to lose him.

When the doctor gave the news, Abbas had only one question: "Was it a boy?"

Seeing the desperation from his rigid face, the doctor consoled him.

"Yes," he said.

Abbas lowered his head and locked himself in the baby's nursery, refusing even to enter the other room in which his wife was sobbing. He stood for hours, caressing the cradle that he had built with his own hands.

He passed the next few nights at his parents' house, in his old childhood bedroom. He didn't talk to anyone; he sat eating in silence or drinking liters of tea that Parì kept bringing to him, as if in a vain attempt to fill the bottomless well of his grief.

It was Hossein who finally shook him out of his misery.

"That's enough, Abbas. I'm ashamed of you. You're not a little boy and you can't keep crying and neglecting your duties as a husband. Your wife needs you. Go to her. Act like a man."

Hossein had never taken this tone with him before, not even when Abbas was a child.

Abbas went to Touran, who had never left her bed, nursed by her mother, barely moving, refusing to eat. Pallid and thin, with her delicate features creased by new wrinkles, she seemed like the ghost of the beautiful girl that had rolled around on the field with her brothers.

"I'm sorry," she said to him as soon as he entered.

Abbas couldn't find the words to console her, or tell her that he was sorry to have left her alone with her grief—that there was nothing for her to be sorry about, it wasn't her fault. His voice died in his throat. His glance fell on his beloved's hands, so fragile and bloodless, and he held them in his own, kissing her long fingers one by one. Only then did the tears, which had caught in his throat, flow freely, and he wept in his wife's arms over the death of their first child.

When Touran became pregnant again, Abbas did not swear that he would be the best father in the world. Actually, while Borna was being born, he was attending a meeting. When his second-born, Arya, arrived, he didn't even wait outside the room where his wife was giving birth because he was moving up the chain of command and was completely absorbed by his work. Or perhaps he preferred to stay far away out of fear of reliving that terrible morning in which his marriage, his life, and his faith in the world had been cracked—though he'd never admit it.

But as soon as he saw Borna in the cradle, Abbas's eyes filled for the first time with a tenderness that he would always have for his children, and his children alone. You'd never expect a man so large, with such broad shoulders and thick, combed hair, to be so tender. Yet despite certain rigidities and an attitude of authority that the military had reinforced in him, he had become a proud father. He taught his children everything he had taught his brothers, and much more. He almost never let impatience win, even if the passing years made him more severe. He wasn't the best father in the world, but he was a good one.

Naturally he passed on to his children his respect for the shah and demanded that they stand up and perform a military salute every time the national anthem played. His eyes filled with pride the day when Arya, only four years old at the time, hearing the anthem on the radio, rose to his feet, stood at attention, and stared fixedly at the portrait of the shah. In the middle of the anthem, however, he turned toward his father, terror creeping into his eyes: "*Baba*, I need to go to the bathroom."

"Wait a second, Arya, wait until the anthem ends."

"But *Baba* . . ."

"Arya, you know you can't. This is important, it's His Majesty's anthem."

The boy tried to hold it in a little longer but couldn't. Still standing straight, he started to cry from the shame and fear of being yelled at. Touran stiffened in the corner, worried how her husband would react. But Abbas, at the end of the anthem, took his second-born child by the hand and gently led him to change his clothes. Then he sat his son on his lap and whispered in his ear: "Don't worry," he said, "you urinated in honor of His Majesty."

A FEW MONTHS AFTER ARYA, Alì was born, the belated and unexpected fruit of Hossein and Simin's long marriage. Simin had been severely tested by the pregnancy; she spent all nine months in bed, laid prostrate by her unexpected tumescence and the constant back pain. It took her a long time to recover from the physical strain and she entrusted the baby to the care of Parì, who seemed to rediscover, with that child in her arms, her forgotten passion for children. She attended to his every need, she fed him, she followed him while he ran into the garden and passed entire afternoons playing with him. Parì was her little brother's principal companion and acted almost like his mother, doing everything short of picking up his medical prescriptions. She was the only one who could—Hossein had to work in the bazaar, and Simin had to keep after the other boys: Javad was constantly developing new interests and was never at home, Abbas had his own family and work took up much of his time.

As if aware of being an unexpected guest, Alì grew up docile and taciturn, trying to cause as little trouble as possible. He rarely cried, he obeyed without protest, and, habituated to being alone, he got lost in thought. Parì often found him frozen in a position in which she had left him hours earlier—a drawing pen in hand and a new coloring book, still untouched, open in front of him.

5

Two Brothers

HOSSEIN SUFFERED A CORONARY and died suddenly in the summer of 1968. I was with my family outside of Tehran and didn't get the news until a month later. When my mother and I went to visit the family, Simin seemed much older. She roamed around the house, twisting her hands and staring at us absently. Holding hands with Ali, she looked like his grandmother.

"I didn't think I'd have to spend my last years without him," she kept saying. "What will I do without Hossein? God protect me!"

As soon as we were alone, Pari told me that her mother had showed no sign of recovering. Every task had become insurmountable for her, and she relied on her daughter to handle every chore. Abbas finally took the situation into his own hands, with his usual efficiency. He had been a good son and a good older brother, and now he was a good paterfamilias, ready to take responsibility for his mother and the others. He asked his uncle to take over for his father in their business, because Javad had recently committed himself to the study of engineering and Ali, of course, was too young. The house, of which Hossein was so proud, now seemed too large and extravagant: it was put up for sale and purchased, with a generous offer, by the general who had become Abbas's benefactor. The proceeds were sufficient to buy a small apartment in the same neighborhood and to assure

Simin of a modest living income. So Simin was forced to give up her rose garden and the small plot where she cultivated fava beans, eggplants, tomatoes, and radishes. She took with her only some basil plants that she set up on the windowsill in the kitchen; every time she looked at them she shook her head, saddened by those exiled leaves, oppressed by the metal and the glass of the surrounding landscape, which bore absolutely no resemblance to her former garden's luxuriant green pasture.

The new apartment was too small to hold all the furniture from the old house, but Abbas knew that Simin would never agree to sell any of it. So he managed to cram it all in, filling almost every space in the apartment, including the corners and the hallway. No one complained when, in the half-lit apartment, they stumbled over a low side table or a decorative linen chest. The look on Simin's face when she leaned on the old wood and caressed the sinuous, meticulously dusted forms of the furniture was too poignant. And no one protested the least bit when Abbas explained that it was necessary to sign over to her their inheritances, because the law permitted a woman to inherit only a small amount of the husband's estate—certainly not enough to ensure her a peaceful life.

"What will *maman* do when you get married? She won't have anything."

Parì and Javad, persuaded by their brother's words, ceded their part of the inheritance, while Alì's remained intact, since he was still a minor and unable to manage his own money. The child observed silently these exchanges, without knowing whom to ask for an explanation. In the grief and agitation of those days, he'd been tossed back and forth between various relatives, but wherever he found himself he felt like a guest who had appeared at an inopportune moment. In the new apartment he even lost the right to his own room and ended up sleeping in Javad's. He obediently brought with him his few possessions and the toys that had belonged to his brothers, and he understood that it would be years before he'd have a space all to his own.

Abbas also sent his mother a portion of his own salary: every month he divided it into four parts, keeping three for himself and giving one to her. Furthermore he divided the food rations that the military provided to its officers into two parts, one for his mother and his brothers, and another for himself, his wife, and their two children. When she began again to receive guests, Simin customarily offered, on her most splendid serving tray, the chocolate bars that he had given her.

"Take one. I just got them from my son. They're from Switzerland."

At that time it was considered very stylish to have in the house something that came from another country, and few allowed themselves this luxury. And naturally she liked to boast about her firstborn, a military official who was so generous by nature.

"You're lucky, Simin, to have a son like Abbas."

"Abbas is a real man, with his head set firmly on his shoulders," her friends repeated.

Simin nodded in agreement, more proud than ever, as the chocolate melted on her tongue.

THESE NEW RESPONSIBILITIES stripped Abbas of his natural serenity. Maneuvering between the bureaucracy, the military hierarchy, his two families, and balancing his family's budget, he had transformed into a more serious man. But his children were one thing, his siblings another. And now he worried that his brothers and sister didn't have enough maturity to oversee their household. For years he had covered for Javad, intervening whenever his brother got himself in trouble, often before their father could find out what had happened. He'd also had to drag Javad out of a few fights. It's not that Javad was violent—he just had an impulsive manner and didn't know how to keep his mouth shut, so he made enemies with classmates and neighborhood kids.

"Can't you get out of your own trouble? Have you still not learned how to keep to yourself?" Abbas would say to his younger brother, realizing that it was of no use.

Javad shook the dust off his pants and lifted his shoulders, without even trying to defend himself. An expression—somewhere between apologetic and defiant—fluttered through his long, almost feminine eyelashes; as a smile played on the corners of his mouth.

"At least next time pick on someone your own size," said Abbas, resigned, eying his brother's narrow shoulders.

But everything changed after Hossein's death. The young soldier, oppressed by the weight of his new responsibility, decided that he could no longer protect his younger brother; Javad would have to learn a few hard lessons. The next time Javad got in a fight, Abbas held back. When Javad emerged, looking at him reproachfully—at least with the eye that wasn't swollen—instead of consoling him, Abbas attacked.

"What did you get out of that, besides a black eye?"

"I defended my ideas. You should be proud of me. It's your job, after all, to use violence to defend your ideas," replied Javad, who became arrogant whenever he was in the wrong. But you couldn't provoke Abbas on the subject of the military.

"My job is to defend my country." He didn't raise his voice but he spoke with a dangerous energy that made his shoulders stiffen.

Javad didn't respond, retreating just in time from the chasm that threatened to open up between them. But the earth had shaken and their bond was now in crisis. Abbas, a man of iron loyalties, was suddenly assailed by the thought that his beloved little brother was becoming a man, and in growing up he was distancing himself from the ideas and principles by which he himself lived. Javad, for his part, concluded that he wouldn't always be able to count on his brother's support.

He began therefore to turn more frequently to his peers—friends who understood him, who split their lives, like him, between home and the university and who, above all, shared the same political beliefs. Javad was still in high school when the father of his best friend was arrested and accused of fighting for the Tudeh, the Iranian communist party. The two boys began to read political pamphlets and became interested in Marxist theory, motivated mostly by its illicitness. The Tudeh had been founded during the Second World War by a group of Marxist intellectuals who had been imprisoned by Reza Shah. The shah's son didn't have enough power to eliminate them, and at first had allowed the party to practice freely. The Tudeh had ties to the Soviet Union or rather, as the militants would say, "There is a fraternal relationship with the Soviet Communist Party"—even though this statement implied submission and obedience. Thanks to Russian support, the party had grown its own base, building consensus beyond the antimonarchist intellectuals in the capital, particularly among the oil well workers in the southern part of the country. But in 1949 the shah blamed the Tudeh for the failed assassination attempt against him and declared them illegal. Even more severe measures were adopted after the fall of Mossadegh, as a way to placate the United States, which at the time was in the middle of the Cold War. The Tudeh continued to operate in shadows, however, and to attract global attention to the shah's dictatorship.

When Hossein was alive, he behaved as he had done with Abbas, choosing to be silent in the face of his second-born son's political ardor, convinced that it was only a phase. Javad's proclamations at the dinner table did not particularly enthuse Hossein, but usually he could silence his son with a few words. Hossein lifted his eyes from the plate and begged him, "No politics at the dinner table, please."

And Javad, who didn't lack a sense of humor, would throw back his head in laughter. Meanwhile Abbas, out of respect for his father, held his tongue and tried to ignore his brother's speeches. Only once did he allow himself to get drawn into a heated discussion, in which both of them clashed with their irreconcilable ideologies. When Abbas realized that he was on the verge of wanting to hit his favorite brother, he got scared, and made a resolution to avoid political debates in the future. Javad, without anyone else to provoke, had to be silent.

But when his own children Borna and Arya became involved, Abbas couldn't hold back anymore.

Javad's imprudence led to the quarrel, but it might have passed without any serious consequences if the times hadn't already been so tense and the two brothers so confused and irritated. For Borna's birthday Javad had given his little nephew a beautiful book illustrated by Samad Behranghi. It was the fable of a small fish who is tired of living in his pond so he goes to explore a stream that leads out into the sea. After various encounters and adventures, the small fish meets other small fish who are fighting to cut the fishermen's nets and liberate their school. By the end of the story this struggle has given meaning to his life:

I am now willing to die, but before I do, I must first learn how to live. When my day finally comes—and it will—I won't be afraid. That's because, from now on, I will devote my life to the lives of others.

But before the little fish is able to continue with them, he is captured by a pelican. The fish decides to sacrifice himself in order to save the others.

That night Borna and Arya asked their father to read them the fable. Abbas read it in his deep, slow voice, watching, out of the corner of his eye, the children, who were slipping farther and farther under the covers.

"I want to travel all over the world and become a hero, too!" Borna said, before succumbing to sleep.

Abbas felt an instinctive pride at his little boy's display of bravado, but when he closed the bedroom door he was struck by a feeling of uneasiness. It wasn't the fable's central metaphor that bothered him—he'd never be able to understand that the shah was the pelican, because in Abbas's eyes the shah was no oppressor. What bothered him instead was the independent spirit of the little fish, who went off to explore the world despite the exhortations of the adults, who told him to stay put like all the others. The more he thought about it, the more it seemed to him to be a negative example: What if his children should become deaf to the advice of adults and so stubborn that they lost respect for tradition? This, after all, was the route that Javad had taken: no one had stopped him before it was too late. Abbas had defended Javad when he was acting out as a kid, but the result was that he had now become a spoiled, bratty young man who went around challenging their leader like some kind of freedom fighter. No, Abbas promised himself before going to sleep, he wouldn't make the same mistake with his own children.

The next day, while Borna and Arya were in school, he returned the book to Javad.

"Why don't you just keep it. I don't think it's suitable for the children. In the future I'd prefer that you consult with me before giving them a gift. You obviously don't understand what kind of impression these things can make on a small child."

Abbas's children were the only ones he loved more than the shah. Javad, who truly was still the same irresponsible little boy as always, didn't understand Abbas's anger. Javad could only guess that his brother thought him to be a bad influence on his nephews. This upset him.

"Are you afraid that Arya and Borna might finally snap out of it?" he asked, with a sarcastic grin. He made no move to take back the book but glared at his brother defiantly.

"My children don't need to snap out of anything. They're well educated and intelligent. How dare you judge them?" Abbas hissed, feeling himself on the verge of throwing a punch.

"No one doubts *their* intelligence," responded Javad.

Abbas's open hand landed loudly on his brother's cheek. The sound of the slap resounded through the room. The two men froze, staring at each other, both stunned by the sudden act. The rift that broke between them after the death of their father had become, in a single instant, an abyss so vast that it would swallow every bit of affection they had ever shared with each other.

Javad, his eyes blazing with anger and humiliation, abruptly turned around and walked out. Abbas stayed unmoving, still holding the book in his hand. Only many years later did he learn that his brother, that very same afternoon, made contact with the Tudeh.

6
In the Name of the Shah

"I'M NOT COMING, but you should go," said my father, when my mother proposed a visit to Simin. In the last month, making various excuses, he had always refused to accompany her there.

"I beg you, Mohammad Alì *khan*, don't say that. What will people think if, on feast day, I should abandon my husband and go to another house?"

"Then stay with me, *khanum*," he calmly replied.

"You can play *takteh-nard* with Javad. He's no slouch." My mother was pressing him.

"He's just a boy. If he doesn't win right away, he gets tired and distracted. It's no fun."

The truth was that, since Hossein's death, my father had become terribly bored by our regular meetings with their family. We had begun to spread out the interactions and visit the family separately. My mother still saw Simin and I continued to meet up with Parì. We only heard news about Abbas, Javad, and Alì sporadically.

Usually Parì and I would make dates in the city to chat with other friends at the Café Naderì, ordering *affogato al caffè*, which Parì was obsessed with. By this point I had finished my studies and had begun my apprenticeship as a judge.

That afternoon, when Parì came over to pick me up at my office, she raised an eyebrow in disapproval of my appearance. At the time my attire consisted of whatever clothes I grabbed out of the closet when I woke up, my eyes still full of sleep.

"You work too much," said Parì, shaking her head.

"It's demanding, sure. But I like it."

"Don't tell me that's *why* you like it."

"No—but that's part of it. I just always feel like I don't have enough time to get everything done."

"Come with me—I'll show you what a good time is."

She then dragged me on a marathon tour of shop windows, until we stopped to rest and restore our energy in a *chelow kebabi*, where Parì satisfied her desire to review all of our past culinary experiences. Her stories were lively and even though by now I knew them all by memory, I couldn't help but laugh. Still, every time that I tried to change the subject to politics—a subject that, because of my job, had assumed a certain importance in my life—Parì shrugged. The topic bored her.

"How can it? Didn't you see that, just yesterday, they arrested ten students?"

"My father's right. It's better to stay out of it completely."

I didn't understand this superficial attitude, especially in a woman as intelligent as she was.

Something in her voice, however, betrayed a note of anxiety. Though I almost never went home with her, that night I did.

As we relaxed and had tea in Simin's cluttered sitting room, I noticed a newly strident tone right away.

"A portrait of Esfahan?" I asked her, out of curiosity. I had lifted a small painting from its nail and held it up to the light. It had been a few months since I'd gone to her house and I was surprised to see, amidst her mother's solid wooden furniture, such a trivial object.

"Ugly, isn't it? It's Javad's latest discovery."

I looked at Parì closely. She sighed and let herself collapse on the divan.

"All he does these days is think about his beloved leftist ideas. And anyone who believes otherwise is an enemy."

"I didn't realize he was so dedicated to the cause."

"Me neither, not until recently. But now he never misses an occasion to fight with Abbas. He accuses him of being a conservative, an enemy of the Iranian people. You can imagine Abbas's reaction. Most of the time he just walks out, slamming the door behind him."

I began to understand the source of Parì's antipathy to politics.

"His most recent provocation," she continued, "was to remove the shah's portrait from the house and replace it with this landscape picture. Abbas, when he saw this, started yelling. He called him an ingrate, said that it was only because of the shah that we had a house. He said he refused to waste his time on such nonsense. It got so bad that Abbas said he couldn't believe that he had taken care of Javad all these years. Javad said, 'You know what I think about your money and your ideas?'"

"I can't believe it. They always worshipped each other."

"Not anymore. Abbas walked out, swearing that he'd never step foot in a house that didn't have a portrait of the shah. *Maman* begged him to calm down, but he refused to listen. And Javad was even more difficult. Abbas didn't show up for a month; he sent us money through Touran. Even Borna and Arya were denied permission to come see us."

"Have they made up yet?"

"Not on your life. *Maman*, sobbing, convinced Abbas to return, but he refused to see Javad. He doesn't even want to say his name—he refers to him as 'that one.' He asked me to let him know when Javad is out of the house, so that he can come by without running the risk of crossing paths with him. Can you believe that three months have passed like this? Well, perhaps it's better this way. *Maman* can't see them fight, it breaks her heart."

Some time later, during a family visit with Simin, we saw Abbas. He had just been promoted to general. It was August 19, the anniversary of the coup d'état, and he didn't miss his chance to repeat the story of the pen and the punishment of the traitor.

"First of all, Mossadegh wasn't a traitor, he succeeded where Reza Shah failed: he nationalized the oil industry and fought to free us from foreign influence. It was your shah who permitted the United States to meddle in our businesses. And second, he was a legitimately elected prime minister who was beloved by the people. The Majlis disposed of him, after all—it wasn't the shah, and certainly not the CIA."

Abbas went into a tirade: "I didn't realize that you'd been brainwashed, too! You of all people attack the shah when it's only thanks to him that you can go to a university and become a judge. You know that without the Pahlavi, Iranian women—God bless them—would still be locked up at home, hoping their husbands didn't forget about them?"

Reza Shah had understood the importance of modernizing the country, and he'd sent many young people to study abroad in Europe, to become the professors of the future intellectual elite. Curiously, some of them became the most bellicose opponents of the monarchy, like Taghi Arani, the founder of the Iranian left who was one of the first proponents of Marxist ideology, and

Mehdi Bazargan, the man nominated for prime minister on the day after the Islamic Revolution. The youth who had been educated in Europe ended up teaching at the first modern Iranian university, which Reza Shah had built for Tehran, and which was open to women. The son, furthermore, introduced universal suffrage in 1963. But all of this seemed to me hardly enough to make up for more than forty years of their regime, and to justify Abbas's offensive words.

"I worked hard at the university and earned my position. I don't see why I should be grateful for the shah. If he had been less beholden to the United States, he would have been able to make better use of the oil revenues and he'd stop buying so many weapons. In fact, what we need in Iran is—"

Abbas didn't allow me to finish.

"The weapons protect us against the communists! Have you forgotten the giant that sleeps along the border? What do you think, that the Soviet Union will just leave us in peace? Were it not for the shah and the United States, Mossadegh would have weakened Iran and we would have fallen, like a ripe apple, into the hands of the communists. That which you insist upon calling the coup d'état was a legitimate alliance between the United States and Iran, the most powerful country in the Middle East. Don't you see all the progress we've made?"

I stared at him with fury and sadness: how many other officials had he heard expressing these very same sentiments, even in the exact same words? I had deep respect for Abbas, but all of a sudden he appeared to me as he was: a man of limited intelligence, who allowed others to do his thinking for him.

Abbas continued:

"I don't understand how anyone who attends a university can leave with these subversive ideas. Are all of your professors communists? And why don't the administrators prevent the spreading of this kind of propaganda? Look how Javad has been reduced—he now spends more time with his friends than at the university. But it won't ever happen to my children. I'll have them go to school in America. I'd rather have them far away from me than to hear them say, some day, that Iran could do without His Majesty."

My mother gave me a light nudge with her elbow and I changed the subject. I had a better understanding now of why Simin and Parì were so exasperated by politics and by the constant domestic quarrels. After contributing to the escalation of enmity between the two brothers, my own uneasiness grew. It seemed an omen for an impending disaster.

7

Four Gray, Smooth, Bare Walls

ONE AFTERNOON PARÌ called my office and said she wanted to see me as soon as possible. I made an appointment to meet her at Café Naderì, but when I went to leave the court I found her waiting for me at the door.

"I'm sorry, Shirin *joon*," she said, without bothering to exchange any formalities. "I thought better of it. I don't think a public place is such a good idea." She wore large, shapeless pants, an old shirt, and sneakers. I'd never seen her so shabbily dressed, not even at home.

Parì followed my glance. "Today it's your turn to make fun of my sloppy clothes, huh?" But it was a weak attempt at a joke and the smile died immediately on her lips, which were pale, lacking their usual lipstick. "Come, let's take a stroll in the park and I'll tell you what's happened."

We proceeded slowly toward a small strip of grass that only the most generous observer would identify as a park. Parì seemed lost in her thoughts. I was headed toward a small seat in one corner of the area, but she patted me lightly and indicated that she preferred to walk. I waited a few minutes before she began to speak.

"Have you heard about the student protest at the university?"

she asked, to my surprise.

"No, I'm afraid not. What's it about this time?"

"The increase in the cost of bus tickets. The student associations have organized a national strike. You know how it is—the crisis, inflation, exploitation of the people—all the usual things. Javad took part in it." She sighed, shaking her head. "Anyway, the shah canceled the rate increase, but then he decided he'd better arrest all the demonstrators. They took Javad."

"Oh no. How is he?" I didn't know what else to say.

"I have no idea. They're not letting us get in contact with him. They told us only that they've put him in solitary isolation. *Maman* does nothing but cry and pray, cry and pray."

"I'll get my mother to go visit her, so at least she can have some company."

"Thanks, Shirin, you're very nice." She hesitated a second before speaking again. "Actually I'm here to ask you a big favor. You don't know anyone who could help us, do you? Someone who at least could find out something about his case, if only to calm my mother down a little?" Parì chewed nervously on her lip. I understood how much it pained her to involve me in this.

"Parì, you know that if I could help, I'd do so happily. But what I do in court has nothing to do with this kind of thing, and I don't know anyone. The opposition are 'special' prisoners and they aren't processed through the usual channels."

"Of course. I'm sorry. It's just I don't know where to turn. I'm really worried." We were at a standstill. When Parì looked me in the eye I could see that she hadn't been sleeping.

"Have you spoken with Abbas? He must know somebody."

"The short answer is that he doesn't want to do anything. He says that it's about time Javad learned to take care of himself.

Abbas can't keep saving him from trouble. That's my brother for you, our family's great protector." Her voice trembled with anger.

"Perhaps he's worried about his career. If his superiors discovered that he's related to a communist—"

"No, that's not what it's about. Or perhaps it is—maybe he's worried, and he's just not admitting it. I'm afraid that he's ashamed of Javad, that he's humiliated to have a 'rebel' for a brother. And deep down he thinks that Javad deserves to be locked away in prison."

AT THE TIME I couldn't really understand what it meant to be locked away in a solitary cell. But thirty years later, I would discover what it was like firsthand.

The door closes behind me with a hard click. *I find myself in a small room, measuring about three by two meters. Four gray, smooth, bare walls. From the ceiling there hangs a lightbulb that emits a faint glow. There are no windows. The floor is covered with wall-to-wall carpet encrusted with dust and excrement—it appears not to have been washed for years. More likely it's never been washed. It's so dirty that I can't even tell what color it is.*

Piled in a heap in one corner is a rough cloth blanket: it seems somehow even dirtier than the carpet. A spoon and a bowl of milk, belonging to some previous inmate, completes my inheritance.

I look around for a long time, disheartened. I don't dare touch anything. Infections and diseases—even AIDS—are common in prison. I have a husband and two daughters waiting for me at home, I'm afraid that I'd infect them with something.

At first I don't know what to do, I stand frozen for more than two hours, drawing upon all my reserves of energy to delay the moment when I will have to sit down. But I begin to get very tired. Who told me that I'll be set free? I ask myself. And if I have to stay here, why not just give up?

As soon as I have this thought I collapse, exhausted, to the ground. I hug my knees and bow my head to hide my tears. What had I done to deserve this?

One night, while a group of students from the University of Tehran protested the closing of a progressive newspaper, the police and the lebas-shakhsi entered the dormitory, wounding a number of kids and killing one of them, Ezzat Ebrahimnezhad. I was the lawyer chosen by his family to discover and convict whoever had ordered the assault, and the person who had opened fire. My research proceeded well enough and I had found one person who was willing to testify. The witness had evidence of everything he alleged and wasn't forced to retract anything, but the court chose to incriminate me for having entered false testimony rather than listening to his testimony. It was never a good idea to accuse the police of anything in the Islamic Republic of Iran.

My cell faces an empty corridor. There is no sound around me, no weeping, no breath. The absolute silence puts me in a panic and constricts my stomach. I'd pay in gold just to have someone talk to me, remind me I'm alive, that there's still a whole world of human beings somewhere out there.

Even in sleep I can't find peace. I don't have a cushion and when I ask for one, the guard tells me that it's not permitted. So I sleep with my arm folded under my head, but after an hour it's completely numb and I awake from the pain. When my arm's not numb,

I feel my sciatica acting up. In prison, for whatever reason, you're not allowed to wear socks. The humidity agitates my inflammation and I turn over for hours without finding a position that can offer me any relief.

Time seems not to pass, or perhaps it passes too quickly. Soon I lose all awareness of hours and days. The light always stays on and without a window it's impossible to know when it's night and when the sun is out. When they arrested me they confiscated everything I was carrying: a pen, notebook, glasses, and, of course, my watch. That was the worst of it—they confiscated time. How to pass it and how to measure it. I desperately needed to reason, to take account of things, to know what time it was and how much time had passed since my arrest. I know that whenever they bring me bread, cheese, and tea, it's a new day, or at least I've convinced myself that it's breakfast. But soon I begin to suspect that they're deliberately substituting dinner for breakfast to make me lose track of time and go insane. I worry that they're succeeding.

Once in a while the peephole opens and from the outside a guard watches me without saying a word, only to humiliate me and see me fall deeper and deeper into despair.

The first days those indiscreet, searching eyes infuriate me. They violate my meager sense of privacy. But soon I remember that they've installed video cameras in the isolation cells to monitor the movements of the detainees. One day, after a long search, I find it, above the hinges of the door. I explode in laughter and, upon hearing the hoarse, withering sound that escapes in bursts from my mouth for several minutes, I think I'm on the edge of madness. Right after that, a sense of discomfort comes over me. The certainty of being observed makes it even more difficult to bear this life. Now I feel embarrassed every time that I undress and change clothes, I can't cope with the idea that strangers, probably men, can see my naked body. Even just staying seated, drinking from the bowl, or eating, causes me embarrassment. I force myself not to cry, so as not to give satisfaction to those on the other side. And this is my salvation, because the stubbornness of my desire not to let them win is what saves me from succumbing to despair.

Once a week a female guard leads me out of the cell to take a shower. She stays with me while I undress and wash myself under the hot jet. Not even there can I have a moment of privacy. The next day I'm forced, without gloves, to wash my cell, the bathroom, the bathtub, and the corridor. With that glimmer of rational thought that still gives resistance, I try to convince the guards to have the cleaning done before I take my shower rather than after, but it's not possible to alter this absurd torture. So I have to get myself dirty and remain dirty for a full week, then go through the whole thing all over again.

Every night a different guard brings me into the interrogation room. Every night, always the same questions that I've answered hundreds of times. No one hits me, but sometimes I even think that it would be better if they did, instead of having to submit, again and again, to that same continual barrage of questions.

Only after it's over will I learn that psychologists call solitary isolation "white torture."

JAVAD REMAINED IN PRISON for a year. Parì and his mother won permission to see him a few times; though after every encounter they left the prison destroyed. Simin went to bed moaning, or praying, banging her head for hours against the *mohr*, the "seal," the small flat section of terra cotta used by the Shiites for prayer. Parì wandered through their house like a sleepwalker, alternately against "irresponsible Javad" and "pig-headed Abbas."

Ultimately the persistent recriminations of the mother and sister and, above all, their tears, convinced Abbas. He called one of his friends who, using maximum discretion, spoke to some higher ups. Javad was released without knowing to whom he owed his freedom.

8

Mashhad

JAVAD SEEMED LIKE a new person: lanky and extremely thin, with a serious, penetrating gaze that made you uneasy. His speech was erratic, with long pauses between words, as if he were out of breath. He also had asthma. They'd broken his nose, and it was still twisted. His right cheekbone had a considerable scar that began at his ear and extended to his lips. He couldn't walk by himself because it hurt him to stand. In prison they had whipped the soles of his feet as a form of torture: as soon as the wounds showed signs of healing, they'd reopen them with more violent lashes.

Simin was so happy to have her son back home that she chose not to dwell on his condition and instead dedicated herself to transforming him back to how he was before prison. She dusted off her magic culinary utensils and organized a large family lunch, serving all of Javad's favorite dishes. Javad, accustomed to prison food, barely managed to swallow a few mouthfuls. Abbas, of course, refused to participate, not wanting to violate his policy of avoiding contact with his brother.

"We had leftovers for a week, me and Ali," Parì said, laughing. "Javad had little more than a nibble. And to think, some people thought that *maman* had lost her touch!"

But Simin wouldn't give up. She lavished her son with attention. She wanted him to sleep late, to recuperate. She wanted to give him new clothes and the only reason she held back was because of his size: in prison Javad had lost more than fifteen kilograms and she hoped he would regain as much of his previous weight as possible. At the thought of his thin, white body, on which his old clothes hung shapelessly, she decided against it, convinced that whatever she bought would soon be too tight on him.

Javad appreciated his mother's good intentions, but he couldn't tolerate this kind of excessive attention. With some irritation he brushed her off whenever she started giving him suggestions—"Why don't you relax a bit in the armchair? You're still weak, don't you think you should get under the covers? Are you hungry? Look at these wonderful oranges I bought yesterday. Have one, you'll feel better."—and it was only his respect for her that kept him from responding rudely. To avoid Simin's constancy, he spent much time out of the house, wandering about without any specific destination, or he locked himself in his room, stretched out along the horrible wooden board that he'd chosen to serve as his bed. He decided not to reacclimate himself to the comforts of his past: because prison had revealed to him his future, it had made him understand his duty to oppose the regime. If this battle was his destiny, sooner or later it was likely that he'd be forced into hiding or arrested again: better then to be prepared and train himself right now, in body and spirit, for the trials of another detention—so this meant adapting his bony back to the wooden board.

After prison he felt like a man: he had submitted to his isolation and reclusion in silence, he had forgotten hunger, he had resisted torture. Everything that he had liked previously—soccer games and talking with friends—no longer interested him. They were habits that belonged to another world or, rather, to another person: the little boy that he once had been. He responded, therefore, with total indifference to the letter of expulsion he received from the university. At this point it made no sense to return to classes, it would be a waste of time and a negation of everything that had transpired.

He began to look for a job and responded to all of the help-wanted ads, but no matter how low he set his terms, he kept getting turned away. Finally he realized that the problem was his prison sentence, and it'd be difficult to find anyone who would give him a second chance, at least in Tehran. He was certain this would always be the case: wherever he went, the secret police would be keeping an eye on him. The man reading the newspaper on the park bench, the doorman down the block, even the shop boy who had been making deliveries to Simin for years—all of them, without exception, could be spies working for the Savak.

SIMIN ORGANIZED A THREE-DAY TRIP to Mashhad, the central city in Khorasan Province, on the border with Turkmenistan. It is the resting place of Reza, the eighth imam, who died in 817 after having eaten poisoned grapes—that's the legend at least. After his death, what was a humble village was transformed into the most important holy site for Shiites; for twelve hundred years it has been visited by millions of pilgrims. Kings and sultans for centuries have vied to build the greatest tribute to the sacred place, erecting cupolas, mosques, and minarets in a sparkling exhibition of magnificence that has no equal in the entire Middle East. Today every street converges at the sanctuary, surrounded by circular walls that enclose within them two mosques, six theological colleges, two museums, four courtyards, offices, and libraries.

A great center of religious studies, Mashhad had been the
site of numerous revolts during the reign of Reza Shah against
those who, like Ataturk in Turkey, promoted the laicization of
the state. Reza Shah had been the first ruler to open the sanctu-
aries to tourists; he also reformed the civil code by adding laws
of European origin, transferred judicial power from the religious ·
leaders to the courts (thereby breaking strongly with Sharia law),
returned the country to its pre-Islamic origins by restoring the
Persian calendar and, in 1935, changing the official name of the
nation from the State of Persia to Iran. The most extreme measure, however, was the prohibition of the veil: in protest, some
exponents of the clergy sought refuge in the sanctuary. But not
even that could stop Reza Shah: the clashes continued beyond the
sanctuary walls, with both sides taking losses.

My mother decided to join their pilgrimage and convinced
me to go along with her. We left the next morning, along with
Simin, Parì, and Alì. I was surprised to see that Javad was absent:
no one had said so explicitly, but it was clear that the purpose of
the trip was to give thanks for his release from prison.

"You know how my brother is," Parì confided in me, as soon
as we were alone. "He thinks that prayer is for the weak and for
fanatics and he doesn't want to have anything to do with it. So
he let *maman* organize the whole thing, and then, at the last
moment, he pulled out. Anyway, I know the real reason why: he's
desperate to have some time to himself."

Upon arriving in Mashhad we were welcomed by the usual
throng of the faithful. Men and women of every age crowded
the streets and moved in a single procession in the same direction, some speaking animatedly, some with their heads bowed in
prayer. They brought to mind a column of ants marching toward

an anthill. Here and there emerged the turbans of the mullahs, who had come from the theological schools; those who were descendants of the Prophet wore black, the rest wore white. We followed the pilgrims to behind the circular walls.

Inside the *haram-e motahhar*, the sanctuary's core, dozens of beggars approached with outstretched hands. Crippled, blind, or impoverished, they lay on the ground in every corner, shielding themselves from the sun with black cloaks.

Simin headed straight for the fountain where the pilgrims washed their hands and feet before entering the sacred areas. As we were doing our ritual ablutions, I was struck by the sight of the large golden cupola that rose above the mausoleum of the Imam Reza, splendid against the sky's azure backdrop. I was still admiring its sharp, luminous shape when Parì nudged me with her elbow.

"C'mon, the others have already gone. I don't want to lose them."

We hurried to catch up with Simin and my mother; Alì followed a little behind them, his head down. We rejoined the ordered procession of pilgrims who every day visited the mausoleum to beg for the imam's protection. As soon as my eyes, dazzled by the sun, grew accustomed to the light inside, I spotted the enormous golden memorial chapel that protected the tomb from human contact. A shiver ran through me in the darkness, as around me I felt the rustling movements of strangers who leaned forward to touch and kiss the wide trellis, and then walked around it several more times, murmuring their prayers. Simin knelt down and clasped her fingers together before the golden spirals, as if to support herself; she pressed her lips against the metal.

Alì, after giving his sister a dirty look, knelt beside his mother. Mother and son remained in that position for a long time, until the throng of pilgrims forced them to rise again.

"C'mon Shirin, let's do our duty and get out of here."

Simin, Alì, and my mother decided they wanted to stay in the mausoleum all day, because it was Thursday, the day on which the *kumail* supplication is recited. Parì accompanied me on an expedition to the *haram-e motahhar*. We visited the Majsjed-e Azim-e Gawhar Shad, the Great Mosque of Gawhar Shad (the wife of Tamerlane's oldest son), who wanted to build an everlasting memorial to her own memory. A vain woman, she dared to ask for a cupola larger than the golden one on the mausoleum; her architects satisfied her desire and constructed an immense structure, fifty meters high, its entire surface paneled in blue porcelain. We looked up at the rich, golden portal and the profusion of marquetry in hard stone until Parì begged me to go to lunch with her—the aroma of the nearby restaurants had a greater pull on her than the fine mosaics.

"Culture just doesn't do it for me, Shirin," she said, dragging me toward the place she'd been wanting to go since that morning. "I know that my mother was going to be insufferable, but I didn't expect you to be so boring, too."

"I didn't realize how religious your mother was."

"She was always that way, but it's been worse since Javad got out. This whole pilgrimage is for him. She wants to beg the imam to look after him. For three months he's been looking for a job without any success. And, between us, I don't think that Imam Reza himself would be able to help."

"You really think the Savak is after him?"

"Javad's convinced of it. He says that in Tehran he'll never find anything. I've begun to look around for him, too. It's not like he's asking for some high level position: he's applied for work as a laborer, but no one's taking. Last month it seemed like he was going to be hired as a sales clerk for a shop that sells electronic parts, but when he showed up for the first day of work, the proprietor changed his mind. The man made it clear to Javad that 'he had no choice.'"

"And his old friends—can't any of them help out?" I asked.

"No one. His buddies from college are looking out for themselves: they have family, jobs, some of them are earning a lot of money and they don't want any trouble. When they see him in the street, they pretend not to recognize him. My brother was the only one who actually believed in what he was doing. And what did he get out of it? A year of prison and asthma," Parì concluded, in a philosophical tone.

"ALL RIGHT, WHERE ARE WE GOING NEXT?" Parì proposed going to Tus to visit the tomb of the poet Ferdousi, author of the epic national poem the *Shahnameh*, or *Book of the Kings*.

But Alì refused to come. "I love Ferdousi, but I love Imam Reza more," he explained, his shoulders set back.

Parì—who for a long time had tried to rekindle the privileged relationship she once had with her little brother, whom she loved and cherished until her obligations at the university had dragged her away—tried to convince him. "Pay homage to Ferdousi a little bit, just as you would honor the fathers of Iran. He knew how to sing of our story and our spirit—unlike your mullahs, who mumble their little prayers in Arabic without even understanding what they're talking about."

Alì suddenly raised his head. "You shouldn't say those things. The mullahs are saints on earth."

"How clever you are, Alì. You know how many mullahs take multiple wives? How many sign a *sigheh*?"

The *sigheh* is a matrimonial contract used when it's necessary to legitimize an alternative form of marriage. It is usually signed in the mausoleums; women offer themselves to the pilgrims in exchange for a modest *mehrieh*—the money due to the wife as compensation for the marriage. After a brief, pro forma ceremony, the couple consummates the union and then each one goes their own way.

"Parì, you shouldn't doubt the words of the mullahs. Just because one of them may do wrong, that doesn't mean that all of Islam is wrong." He left for the sanctuary to join in the prayers.

While the rest of us were walking around the towering monument to the glory of the eighth imam Reza Shah, Parì remained off to one side. I knew her well enough to understand that she was taken aback by Alì's refusal. Hoping that her bad mood would pass, I convinced the others to go for a walk in a nearby park. Finally, after a long silence, Parì found the words for what she wanted to say: "It's really a sin to waste such a beautiful day closed up inside a mosque. Alì's just so stubborn sometimes."

Simin, resentful, came to his defense: "Stop insulting your brother. You could learn from his example. He's only a boy, but he's already a good Muslim, just like his father, God bless him."

Though he had known Hossein the least of all of the sons, Alì bore the greatest physical resemblance to him. Short and compact, he had, since he was a child, walked with the same slow gait— one foot in front of the other, as if he were measuring the earth. Simin said that he had inherited his father's black, penetrating eyes. Unlike him, however, he never joked around and he had no friends. His entire childhood passed in solitude; the constant moving between rooms, the need to avoid disturbing anybody, had marked him. The taciturn baby had become a timid, surly boy, whose experience was limited to the grimmer aspects of life, and seemed irritated whenever anyone laughed too exuberantly. He found laughter unseemly.

He spent entire afternoons praying at the mosque, wearing out his *mohr* with his forehead. He felt at home there; he was well-liked and treated the same as all the other faithful. A mullah had taken him under his wing and gave him the kind of attention that he had never received at home. The mullah helped Alì to read the Koran, he taught him to memorize the suras, and sometimes he took him along when he went on his rounds through the city.

Simin knew he was safe with the mullah and she approved of Alì's religious values, which shielded him from the political manias of his older brothers—or at least so she believed. She thought it was a normal passion, even if no one else in the family had ever been nearly as devoted. Not even Hossein, despite being so faithful and respectful. Abbas was a good Muslim by all appearances but, as Parì would say, he'd more happily pray to his shah. As for her, she prayed only when there was an upcoming exam or when she had something she wanted.

"*Maman*, I promise you, I'll pray next semester," responded Parì, with one of her typical smirks. "I'm on vacation—what do I need to bother Allah with now?"

Simin gave her a fiery glare. She was a true believer, that one.

* * *

THEY CAME BACK FROM MASHHAD to an empty house. Javad was gone. He'd taken his books and his pamphlets, he stuffed in his suitcase whatever old clothes he could still fit into, and he left, leaving behind only a card:

Maman,

There's nothing for me in Tehran. I'm an adult and I can't continue to burden you. And I don't want Abbas to take care of me out of a salary that's funded by taxpayers' money. I'm sorry not to have told you in advance, I just knew that you wouldn't let me leave. I'm meeting up with a friend in Rasht. He told me that there, what with the factories and the port, even someone like me can find a job.

With affection,
Javad

9
Ali's Beard

IN 1963 MOHAMMAD REZA SHAH, on the prompting of the Kennedy administration, launched a series of reforms that came to be known as the *enqelab-e sefidi*—the White Revolution. The objective was to prevent the country from turning toward communism by bringing about a rapid modernization that included such measures as a redistribution of land, the nationalization of agriculture, and reforms in the systems of electoral practice, government administration, and education.

The shah submitted the initiatives to a referendum, which passed by a rather suspicious consensus of 99.9 percent. Religious groups and students boycotted the vote; in response the army occupied the University of Tehran, where hundreds of students protested, shouting, "Yes to reforms, no to the shah!"

With the White Revolution, Mohammad Reza risked alienating a number of allies. The large real estate owners and the mullahs, who were also major property owners, did not at all appreciate the redistribution of land that threatened their secular privileges. Nor did the clergy accept the establishment of an "army of knowledge," a group of young diplomats sent throughout the countryside to teach peasants how to read and write, work traditionally overseen by the mullahs and that assured them a solid base of influence. For their part the merchants didn't support the fiscal policies and the price controls, which they believed would ruin their businesses.

So it happened that in June, for three days, the population went out into the streets to protest. The religious groups were led by the voice of Ruhollah Khomeini, who was brave enough to oppose the shah openly. Though he was arrested many times, he didn't stop his attacks and expressed rage when Mohammad Reza agreed to concede diplomatic immunity to all Americans in exchange for new arms shipments. The shah asked Khomeini to behave with more composure, and ultimately Khomeini's actions resulted in his exile—first to Turkey, then Iraq.

When Prime Minister Hassan Alì Mansur was assassinated by an Islamic fundamentalist who wanted to protest the shah's measures, in particular the concessions granted to the United States, the shah revoked American immunity. But the White Revolution continued. The slightest spark was enough to unleash new protests, which the shah suppressed more bloodily than ever. The demonstrators in 1963 were imprisoned, tortured, and killed.

The enemies of the sovereign fell into three categories: nationalists, who had inherited Mossadegh's liberal ideas; communists, who joined various local organizations; and religious advocates, who were opposed to the laicization of the state and to the emancipation of women. The shah, who owed his power to his support of the United States, observed this first group with the greatest suspicion, fearing that they might align with the American government and overthrow him. It was impossible to imagine that the clerics or the communists might do the same.

But the communists could create an opening for the Soviet Union to install a sympathetic government and thereby have access to the waters of the Gulf. In any case, the Islamic groups appeared the most innocuous: being opposed to the laicization of the State, they could neither align themselves with liberal

America or atheistic USSR. The shah, after exiling Khomeini, adopted less restrictive policies to avoid antagonizing the majority of the Iranian population, who had always been profoundly religious. But he underestimated the influence of the mullahs on the general public: they had the most direct contact with members of all the social classes, especially the lower ones.

In 1977 Khomeini's oldest son, Mostafa, died in Iraq in a traffic accident for which there circulated a variety of contradictory explanations, ranging from simple distraction to assassination. The funeral rites in his honor concluded with a clash between the crowd and law enforcement. The event seemed to light a fuse that would explode the tensions that were being felt throughout Iran. Protests followed, one after the next: The intellectuals demanded freedom, the religious advocates rose up in favor of the exiled Khomeini, and the workers went on strike, testing the strength of the national economy. On September 8, 1978, after a particularly effective demonstration, the shah ordered the military to shoot into the crowd, a day that would henceforth be known as "Black Friday."

Afraid of the power of the religious groups, he tried to further marginalize Khomeini by having him expelled from neighboring Iraq. But the transfer of Khomeini to the Parisian suburb of Neauphle-le-Château worked to his disadvantage, because it gave the Ayatollah a way to transmit his messages through the mass media. In no time at all, he became the only leader recognized by all of the forces in opposition to the shah, who was now faced with the one scenario he had not envisioned, which he couldn't even have imagined—nationalists, communists, and Islamic groups joined in alliance to ruin the monarchy, shouting "The Union To Victory!"

I was part of those protests myself. After years of silence and forced support, I had become optimistic, while at the university, with the conviction that we might be able to accomplish something. Though I had yelled then against the increase in enrollment taxes, by 1978 it seemed that we—that all of us—had the power to change the country. And this made me tremble with pride. With my husband and some friends, we joined the marches and shouted our slogan: "Independence, liberty, the Islamic Republic!" At the time I really believed that an Islamic Republic would bring us independence and liberty.

THE DEMONSTRATION BEGAN at the Ghoba Mosque, near Azadi Square. The procession left at eight and grew larger as it went: small groups flowed in from the side streets along the route and widened the river of people. I soon found myself surrounded by many more than I'd anticipated, men and women raising flags, voices that chanted in unison for renewal.

Some carried a portrait of Mossadegh, others carried Khomeini's. That's the passage of time for you, I thought: the old prime minister was the great hope of the past; now that he was dead, the Ayatollah would take his place.

In a courtyard to our right, a group of Islamists had lined up. A mullah was walking in front, and he was followed by a group of disciples with very short hair and shaggy beards. Alì was one of them. I hadn't immediately recognized him. After Parì went to study for an advance degree in England, I lost contact with their family.

Alì was all grown-up: a large young man, he walked with his head bowed over a photograph of Khomeini. His face, which had once been so sweet, now wore a vexed expression, and a hint of a beard already obscured his cheeks.

"Alì, is that you? How are you? What a glorious day! And Parì—it's been ages since I heard from her, how is she?"

It was prohibitively expensive to dial foreign numbers so we had to make do with a few dull letters about subjects that, by the time they arrived, were ancient history.

"Her last letter," I continued, "came two months ago. Have you—"

Alì interrupted me brusquely. "Sister, the number of Islam's supporters is growing, and even Parì, *inshallah*, will soon return to Iran to serve the people."

His formal, detached tone took me by surprise. "Alì, it's me, Shirin—don't you recognize me?"

He remained silent, his mouth stubbornly closed shut. He stared at a random section of the pavement. Then I understood. He was protesting the fact that I wasn't wearing a scarf. Alì didn't want to commit a sin by looking at a woman without a veil, so he had decided to direct his stare at the street. I was horrified; I couldn't open my mouth. He was fourteen years younger than me—he almost could've been my son. I'd held him in my arms when he was a child, I'd played with him, I'd helped him with his homework. And here he was openly treating me with contempt.

My husband took me by the arm. "Shirin, c'mon, we're falling behind." I followed him, still astonished. Alì resumed his march without saying another word.

I continued to glance at him along the way. Then I recognized his mullah. He had read the prayers during the ceremony that Simin had held to pray for Javad's release from prison. At the time she had confided in me that the mullah had two wives and five children, who shared a poor, two-room apartment. "He's a good man," Simin had said, and his condition pained her, so every month she gave him a little bit of money in place of the ritual offers of *khoms* and *zakat*.

Now that same mullah was walking with a self-assuredness that bordered on haughtiness, shouting, "Death to the shah!" Alì followed him like a shadow.

PARÌ CAME HOME TWO MONTHS LATER, as carefree as ever. She had a silent-movie-era hairdo and had needed to get another suitcase to fit all the new clothes she'd bought.

Alì's behavior had offended me and I couldn't forget it. I told her about it as soon as I saw her.

"Yeah, that brother's become a bore, too," she replied, with a laugh that disarranged her elegant bangs. "That's all we were missing in this family—an Islamic fundamentalist. You know he even spends his nights in the mosque?"

"And what about his emancipated older sister—does he have anything to say to you?"

"Oh, yes, he tries rather hard to maintain 'decorum' at home. But as soon as he begins to proclaim from his rulebook on being a good Muslim, I jump up and hug him. You should see how he tries to run away, disgusted," she said, laughing.

"But you're a grown-up yourself—why do you let him treat you like that?" Once again, Parì's lightheartedness seemed incredible to me, especially when confronted with the unraveling of a bond that had once been so strong, and which I now feared was irreparably torn.

"Maybe I'm the only one who really takes after our father. I always think that family is what counts the most, and everything else will work itself out sooner or later." Parì went back to sipping her jasmine tea, lost in her thoughts.

I wanted to tell her that, unfortunately, Hossein's philosophy had twice been proven wrong by two of her brothers, and Alì was on the verge of proving it wrong a third time. I wanted to say that it was the family itself that was disintegrating.

"Speaking of which, do you know what happened to Javad? He says that it's useless to stay in Rasht now that there's a revolution. He quit his factory job and moved back in with us to 'give a hand to his compatriots.' *Maman* was the picture of joy: all her sons close by. Too bad that my brothers can't be in the same room without fighting. Not a single one of them agrees with each other!"

She gave me a pointed look. "Poor Abbas. Now, in order to enter the house that he helped pay for, he needs to wait until Javad and Alì have left. He can't stand either of them."

As ALWAYS, PARÌ DWELLED on the amusing side of things and held back everything that upset her. Only many years later did she tell me what had happened between her brothers.

During the first months in which Alì had begun to follow the mullah, Javad never let him alone.

"Javad, stop it," begged Alì, who was still a susceptible boy. He slalomed around the old furniture, accelerating his pace from the hallway to the kitchen, to the living room, around the red armchairs and the divan, ending up diving into his bed.

Javad was always a few inches behind him, almost stepping on his heels. "Isn't this what you do with your mullah? Why doesn't it bother him?"

"He's a guide. Of course I should follow him. I learn from him."

"That's ridiculous. You've melted your brain from praying so much."

"Javad, stop it."

"You should think with your head, Alì. Think with your head. And please, cut your beard. I can't look at you like this. Why don't we give you a little bit of a trim?"

Every time Javad saw him he asked the same question, moving his fingers to imitate the scissors. Alì responded only with a groan—he'd given up on trying to give his brother a logical explanation. He wanted it that way and that's all: short hair and long beard. Even if, in actuality, his facial hair was sparse and ragged.

Javad got into the habit of making the same gestures to the mullahs he saw in the street. He'd walk over and, behind the mullah's back, he would raise his index and middle fingers in a sign of contempt. They annoyed him—not the mullahs themselves, though he didn't exactly love them either; no, what he hated were their beards, those long, dirty, hideous, wild gray beards, which covered their entire faces. He felt an overpowering urge to pull them off the mullahs' faces. To resist the temptation he had invented that gesture, an imitation of a pair of scissors, and though he made the movements with his fingers, he didn't say anything, and thus placated his urge.

One night he decided, with his usual impetuousness, that if he couldn't make Alì shave, he would do it himself. He heard Alì come home, undress, lie down. He stayed still in the darkness until he could hear his brother's breathing become rhythmic and heavy. He went into the kitchen, opened a drawer, and removed the scissors without making a sound. Stealthily he approached his brother's bed and bent over him, a centimeter at a time, until he was right next to his head. But as he was raising the scissors a bone in his knee twitched, making a sharp, piercing sound. Alì opened his eyes and screamed.

"What's happening?" shouted Simin, running down the hall like old times, when her young sons had bad dreams and shouted out in the night.

"He's trying to kill me!"

Alì jumped to his feet, covered with sweat. Javad remained crouched, humiliated by the failure of his plan, but he shook his head indignantly at the absurdity of Alì's claim.

"I wanted to give you a little trim. That beard is disgusting, and you can smell it as soon as it comes through the door."

Parì, who had also come running out of her room, burst into laughter. Simin slapped her.

"*Maman*," Parì whimpered, more stunned than upset.

Each brother was slapped, too. Simin glared at them, too furious to talk. They had woken her up in the middle of the night, terrified to death of what might have happened.

She went back to bed, thinking about when they were children and all she had to do to calm them down was hold them in her arms, caress them, and whisper that nothing had happened. Now she felt powerless. To come across one of her sons brandishing a pair of scissors in his own brother's face—that was something no mother could bear.

Allah Akbar

EVERYONE KNEW THAT the shah was gravely ill. The drugs used to keep the tumor in remission were clouding his mind. Though the country was in rebellion, he didn't seem able to take action. He changed his advisors, he accepted some demands, but then he ordered the troops to fire on the crowds. Without adopting any clear policies, his officials no longer understood which orders to follow. Even the United States seemed to have abandoned Iran to its own fate.

Meanwhile the protests increased, the demonstrations became even more prominent, the strikes spread to the national level, and those who had previously been indecisive now began marching in public. The voice of Ayatollah Khomeini on the other side of the world spread the single shout that united all of the factions: "Out with the shah!"

In a desperate effort to win back the public's loyalty, Mohammad Reza said in a televised speech that he had heard the voice of the Revolution and accordingly had nominated Shahpur Bakhtiyar for prime minister. To calm the waters, Bakhtiyar promised to suspend martial law and advised the shah to leave the country temporarily. Even the United States, through their ambassador William H. Sullivan, supported this solution. When Sullivan passed the message to him, Mohammad Reza told him, "OK, but where should I go?" The Americans, his former supporters, didn't want to risk alienating the revolutionaries and pushing them toward an alliance with the Soviet Union.

In the middle of January 1979 the shah left for Egypt, where he visited President Anwar el-Sadat. In the following months he moved from one country to another, but the gravity of his tumor required sophisticated medical treatment. Finally, American president Jimmy Carter, agreed to accept his entry into the United States as a private citizen on October 22, 1979. By that time his health had greatly deteriorated; the shah left the United States and returned to Egypt, where he died on July 27, 1980. His friend Sadat honored him with a state funeral.

In Iran the authorities had closed the airports to try to prevent Khomeini's return, but just two weeks after the shah had left, on February 1, 1979, the Ayatollah landed in Tehran. Whenever he was asked what he was doing, he responded, "*Hicci*"—nothing. The single, sharp word brought profound disappointment to the patriots. Someone justified it by saying it was spoken ironically. But many people greeted him as a liberator. Those who, like me, were unable to make it to the airport to greet him, watched the historic event unfold on television. On February 12 he took control of the military.

For several months, at nine in the evening sharp, everybody— religious followers and communists, intellectuals and the apathetic—leapt to the rooftops of their homes and, following Khomeini's instructions, shouted, "*Allah Akbar*," God is Great. In the diffuse nightlight, the shouts resounded from palace to palace, house to house, in a delirium pregnant with hope and expectation. What would happen to our beloved Iran? No one knew, but the future appeared full of promise.

Khomeini profited from the weakness of the transitional

government to strengthen the positions of the religious leaders and to gather around himself a band of loyal followers. He assumed control of Pahlavi's wealth, with which he maintained the Pasdaran, the new revolutionary guard that he wanted to align with the military. On March 30 and 31, 1979, the population was called to a referendum to vote on whether we wanted to create an Islamic Republic; the resolution passed with an improbable 98 percent of the vote. Khomeini was nominated as Supreme Leader and he quickly assumed full control of the nation.

The new constitution put Iran's fate in the hands of a few people, and it has stayed that way ever since. The Supreme Leader, who was also a religious leader, had effectively gained control of the government's legislative, judicial, and executive branches, and had no need to bother with the Parliament, the people, or any other institution, even though Article 5 established that the people needed to elect the Leader with a majority vote. He is nominated, instead, by the Discernment Council—a body composed of a group of religious extremists popularly elected from a list compiled by the Guardian Council of the Revolution.

The Guardian Council wields enormous power. Without the Council's approval one cannot join the Parliament or be elected president of the Republic. Furthermore the Council has veto power over any law passed by Parliament that it believes to violate the constitution or Islamic principles. Since there have always been divergences of opinion among the various schools of Islam, it's easy for the Guardian Council to justify rejecting any law they don't like. It's no surprise that such a self-referential constitutional arrangement hasn't brought democracy to Iran, nor is it surprising that the Islamic Republic has killed every hope we have had for freedom.

And I don't mean this in a figurative sense. The new regime wanted to clear out every political rival and opposition party, including its old allies. After summary trials that ignored the most elementary rights of the accused—like the right to self-defense—it ordered supporters of the previous government to be shot. Radio, newspaper, and television reports gave extensive coverage to these cowardly homicides, treating them as if they were noble acts. Then came the situation with the Kurds: using the secessionist claims of the Iranian Kurds as a pretext, Khomeini condemned hundreds of people to death. The most egregious insult was to demand that families, in order to retrieve the corpses for burial, reimburse the government for the cost of the bullets used to execute their relatives. Then the Marxist organizations came under attack: first the Mojahedin-e Khalgh, who had made the mistake of waging armed combat, then the members of the Tudeh and the other leftist organizations.

Among the first measures taken by the Islamic Republic's new government to bring about this long-anticipated transformation of Iran were the legalization of polygamy and the decree that women must wear the veil.

THE ONLY PERSON I KNEW who was happy about these changes was Alì. All of his siblings had been defeated, Parì included. When we still believed in the Revolution and sung hymns to Khomeini, she was the only one who said, with eerie prescience, "You'll see, the situation won't get any better. They'll even outlaw the few types of alcohol that we're still allowed to drink."

Alì, however, believed that we were witnessing the fulfillment of his dream for Iran: Khomeini had installed the *velayat-e faqih*,

"Guardianship of the Jurist," an Islamic authority that determined the rights of citizens. What this meant, effectively, was that we would have a government of clerics, the only government—as Alì put it—that was legitimized by Allah instead of by man. Now the *fuqaha*, the virtuous scholars of Islamic code, would govern us; Iran would be transformed into an island of order and morality. Then the Ayatollah would export his political philosophy abroad and reunite, under his rule, all of the Muslim nations, creating the United Islamic States. He was going to create a third superpower, autonomous and independent, new and invincible. Alì worried only that the Ayatollah wouldn't live long enough to realize his grand project—the first thing he did every morning was to find out the condition of the Ayatollah's health.

To achieve his objectives, Khomeini supported the Afghani mujahidin in their revolt against their socialist government. The Soviet Union sent in troops to prevent the fall of the regime but the persecuted mujahidin held their power, becoming the most feared Islamic group. Still unsatisfied, the Ayatollah, in an effort to win over the Lebanese Shiites, supported the founding of Hezbollah.

This was only the beginning of Alì's dream—and many nightmares for the rest of the world.

ALÌ'S MULLAH WAS AN OLD FRIEND of Khomeini's and on the day after the proclamation of the Republic, he was named to the position of procurator general. Up until then the man had been reciting prayers in private homes and living on charity; now he occupied an elite position in the judiciary. And he hadn't even studied law; in fact he didn't even have a diploma. I was disgusted.

Before he took over the position, it had been filled by one of my former professors of jurisprudence, a man of tremendous experience who had been deeply respected. I'd often collaborated with him as a student, helping in his preparation of essays and articles. He had advanced degrees in philosophy, law, and economics; he taught at the university; he wrote about human rights; and he knew English and French perfectly. Outside of his job, he lived a simple life—a man of integrity, he refused to accept bribes. He drove around by himself in an old Peykan; the new procurator, by contrast, had a bulletproof foreign car and was escorted by twenty members of the Pasdaran, as if we were at war. Ali was always right by his side.

The new procurator worked hard to flaunt the importance of his role and the changes he was bringing about. He inspected every office, scrutinizing files that he couldn't understand, simply for the pleasure of giving orders. I met him a few months later, when he was in the middle of this process.

I had been removed from my position as a judge for something over which I had no control: being a woman. After receiving my college degree, a doctorate, and serving ten years on the bench, I was reduced to the level of a secretary. One day while I was working in the office to which I'd been exiled, a colleague informed me that the procurator general was going to make a surprise visit. Judges, staff, even errand boys were expected in the prayer room.

Every time someone said "prayer room" I felt like laughing. During the shah's rule it was called the conference room, and was used mostly for meetings with journalists and to receive special visitors. Now it was where the warriors of faith gathered: Every day at noon, the revolutionaries competed in displays of religious zeal. They rose from their desks with a great din of shifting chairs and they ran into the room, abandoning their shoes in plain sight to make certain that everyone was aware of their presence for the prayers, and they knelt with gusto. They bowed over repeatedly, smacking their heads on the *mohr*, as if a bruise was the only adequate demonstration of their fervor. After ten minutes of urgent, performative prayer, they began ranting against the shah and the United States, shouting empty slogans.

I preferred to pray in the privacy of my home. I'd never entered that room. I stood with a sigh and followed my colleagues. At the door, I removed my shoes like the others. The room was large and rectangular, illuminated by large windows. In the middle of the floor, on an improvised platform, were the chairs for the procurator and his assistant. In front of them, on the right, was a row of seats reserved for the men of the office; to the left were the seats for the women.

I sat down, indignant. I thought of apartheid in South Africa and of racial segregation in the United States. For the first time I understood what it must have felt like to be black.

As my colleagues took their places I began to feel sick. Hygiene, for some strange reason, had been deemed antirevolutionary. Perfumes and deodorants were considered scandalous: the filthiest people considered themselves to be the most ardent supporters of the Republic and of Islam. The stench of feet and stale sweat filled the air, making it impossible to breathe. I wondered how long I'd be able to bear it.

Unfortunately we had to wait another half hour for the procurator to show up. Finally we heard the slamming of four or five car doors, then the heavy gait of military boots pacing through the empty corridors. At last he made his entrance. He gave a rather supercilious wave and stepped onto the stage. The guards arranged themselves in a semi-circle behind him. Two of them remained at the door with their rifles at the ready. The procurator stood up, puffing out his weak chest. That frail little man, so primped up and self-important, seemed a caricature of himself. I made a mental note to tell Parì all about it that night.

He began to sing the praises of the new government, reciting for the umpteenth time the grandiose promises that had been made by the Ayatollah. Every two or three words, he'd throw in an *inshallah* for good luck, as if it were some magic formula. He kept his gaze turned stubbornly on the rows of men, so as to avoid corrupting himself, and also because his beliefs dictated that women didn't deserve a single kind word.

After the small-talk came the threats: the era of the shah was over, criminals and miscreants would be shot. It was the duty of every good Iranian to dedicate himself to his country and thus to earn, *inshallah*, a place in paradise. Whoever didn't obey the rule of the state would be eliminated.

I was filled with disgust. But the thing that really made me ill was to see Alì at his side, nodding vigorously at his boss's every statement.

A Wedding

"*MAMAN,* YOU WANTED ME to get married so badly. Well, here's your daughter-in-law, Fariba."

"Hello," said Fariba nervously.

Simin froze for a second before she greeted her daughter-in-law in a faint voice.

"Javad hasn't told me anything—a little strange that I didn't know I had a daughter-in-law until today, no?" Simin's disapproval couldn't find hiding.

Javad pushed Fariba ahead of him down the hallway, glancing toward the living room where Parì was laid out on the divan, reading a book. He snuck quietly over to his sister, like he was playing some big practical joke, and after taking a deep breath, he exclaimed, "Sister, meet my wife!"

"Have you gone insane? You scared me. Where'd you come from—?" Parì jumped to her feet, shaking her short bob, as if to wake herself up. Then she looked at her brother to try to see whether he was serious.

Javad grinned and turned to Fariba, a tiny, thin girl who had remained planted in the middle of the living room, anxiously clenching her hands together. Parì looked her over from head to toe, then realized that she was staring at the poor girl without saying anything. She assumed her usual festive self.

"Hi! So nice to meet you! I can't believe my brother's found someone willing to put up with him." And she threw her arms around Fariba.

She called me that afternoon: she wanted to see me so she could tell me about her brother's brilliant idea.

"A wife, just like that, without saying anything to anybody. How could he? He knew that *maman* would be upset. She locked herself in the kitchen and didn't come out for hours. I found her drinking tea and eating pastries, staring out the window. She was talking to herself. It wasn't easy to persuade her to come out to the living room."

"Has she made up with Javad?" I asked, intrigued.

"Not yet, but it'll pass. She's grumbling a lot but ultimately she always forgives—especially when it comes to Javad. Besides, what can she do? They're already married. That girl is her daughter-in-law. It's pointless to start an argument now. They'll be enough time for that anyway," Parì concluded, with a wink.

"How long has Javad known her?"

"Since he came back to Tehran. One or two months at most—"

"That seems impossible," I interrupted. "Did Javad really get married so fast?"

Parì nodded, mechanically stirring a spoon in her cup of tea.

"I can see why Simin is so angry," I said.

"It's not that she wanted to choose a wife for Javad," Parì explained, "but she did want at least to spend some time with her first. To get to know the girl, to learn about her family, to plan everything so that it all went smoothly, with a nice ceremony like the one that Abbas had. I bet she'd figured out the menu a long time ago.

"I think," she added, "that she feels a sense of guilt about our father. Since his death, my brothers have gone their separate ways. Each one has doubled down on a different position and they can't even be in the same room as each other for five minutes without arguing. It's as if . . . well, you see, it's as if each one of them has locked himself in a golden cage—beautiful, strong, and as safe and secure as any ideology. But it's still a cage, and they can't see out of it or communicate with each other.

"If our father were still alive," Parì continued, shaking her head, "perhaps he'd know how to smooth out the differences between them. *Maman* is incapable of this, and she feels guilty about it."

There was an uncharacteristically melancholy note in the voice of my radiant, irreverent friend. I tried to distract her.

"So what are Javad and his wife going to do now?"

"Next week they're moving into their apartment."

"And what do you think of her—Fariba?"

"Um . . . she's OK." She was holding back. "She's gracious, a bit timid for sure, but kind, and calm. *Maman* says that those narrow flanks of hers won't make things easy when it comes to having a baby, but give her a few days and she won't think about it anymore. Oh well," she concluded, with a note of optimism, "it could've been worse."

But I knew her too well—the sentiment sounded forced, as if her words were going against her thoughts. It was only at the end of the visit that Parì began to speak freely. "This probably seems silly to you, but at first I was afraid of Fariba," she confided to me in a whisper. She had a guilty expression on her face, as if she was confessing some fantasy of which she was ashamed. She raised her hands. "Don't get me wrong, it's not that I'm the typical jealous, or overprotective, sister. It's just that—well, as soon as I saw her, in that white, almost phosphorescent blouse, and with her jet-black hair, I thought that she was some kind of phantom. It was probably an effect of the light, I don't know, maybe because she's small and as silent as a specter—but she stood there so unnaturally still, in the middle of the room. . . ."

I looked at Parì in surprise. It wasn't like her to be so superstitious.

Blushing a little, she said, "I'm becoming a pretty mean sister-in-law, huh?"

"SHIRIN *JOON*, WHERE ARE THE FLOWERS?" my mother asked.

"I didn't get them, *Maman*," I responded impatiently. "You know that Javad thinks it's a bourgeois tradition. Do you wanna make a scene?"

"Come on, just do it! If he doesn't want them, let's get them for Simin: it'll make her happy that at least *we're* respecting tradition." After my mother had dismissed every objection I had she began gathering a bunch of lilies.

Simin, who had not resigned herself to her son's spontaneous wedding, organized a party to introduce Fariba to relatives and friends. Javad opened the door in jeans and a sweater like usual. I handed him the flowers and before he could say a word, I told him, "Just take them. Besides, you're the bourgeois one here."

He burst into laughter.

"Come Fariba, let me introduce you to that bulldog I told you about." He was referring to the discussions that had become a motif of our adolescence. Once he started reading the Tudeh's pamphlets, he became a conceited little boy who loved to have debates with his contemporaries in which he held forth from the lofty heights of his political consciousness. His understanding of these issues was hardly rigorous but nevertheless it was always superior to that of his friends and of mine, as I didn't care too much about political parties and ideologies at the time. But I couldn't tolerate his pedantic tone and over time I learned enough to be able to respond to his views, and even developed a certain talent for flustering him.

Fariba stood right beside him. She was as tiny as Parì had described her. She must have been about the same age as Javad, but her round shape and her clear complexion made her look like a little girl. She was dressed in jeans, with a simple white shirt that accentuated her long black hair. She was kind and polite, but a little restless. I reprimanded myself privately: I'd allowed myself to be influenced by my friend's bizarre superstitions.

Fariba greeted me, smiling timidly, and followed Javad into the living room. Simin had prepared a spectacular meal: laid out on every possible surface were plates of meat on spits, bowls of yogurt and saffron rice, and various types of *khoresh* and pastries. But there were only a few guests seated on the couch and chairs—some old friends and the closest relatives. Even Abbas and his family were absent. Alì sat on the edge of a chair, apart from the others.

Javad went over to pick on him.

"Hey, Alì, where's your mullah?"

Realizing that he wasn't going to respond, Javad continued, "When are you and your beard going to come visit me? Actually, would you mind coming alone? I don't want any dirty goatbeards in my house."

Alì, irritated, put down his glass of cherry syrup and walked away, and Javad went back to Fariba.

My mother and I took advantage of the pause in the conversation to find Simin in the kitchen. She dried her hands on her apron and greeted us with a hug.

"Have you met my daughter-in-law? A fine girl, no? Though no good Iranian girl should be married like this—in secret. Poor darling, she must have just wanted to make Javad happy. It was all his idea, you see. Didn't even say a word to me." Simin, exasperated, shook her head. There was a harmonious quality to her speech, which went against the agitation of her thoughts. "Have you seen how few people came? They're all offended because we didn't say a word to anyone about it. But I was too ashamed to tell them that there hadn't even been a *khagestari*—a formal request for the bride's hand in marriage. Allah protect them— they didn't have a ceremony. Javad didn't even give her a copy of the Koran or the gold coins. And the *nabat*—how can you begin a life together without the sugar crystals? I don't even want to think about the actual wedding. Knowing Javad, there probably wasn't even a mullah present."

I left my mother to console Simin and joined the others in the living room. Parì was trying to carry the conversation, but her jokes vanished into the void.

PERHAPS SIMIN WAS RIGHT: just three years later, Fariba and Javad's marriage was in trouble.

I saw them at the funeral of Nader, Hossein's brother. He had died from a heart attack while in the middle of praying. Just one

month earlier his only son, Morad, had been executed for having collaborated with the Mujahidin-e Khalgh, the "Army of the
People"—religious extremists faithful to Marxists principles and
opposed to being governed by clerics. As soon as the clerics took
over, they ordered a massive purge of the Mujahidin-e Khalgh; in
1981 they tried to eliminate every member of the party. Having
made a full declaration of war, the mujahidin allied with Saddam
Hussein's Iraq, antagonizing the Iranian people and effectively
signing their own death sentence.

The new regime forbade a funeral service for Morad, so Nader's funeral became an occasion to commemorate both father
and son. The mosque was unusually crowded and outside the
Pasdaran had set up a huge barricade, ready to intervene at any
sign of disorder.

From a distance of several meters, I spotted Simin with her
children and relatives. People lined up to give their condolences.
The men's faces were visible, but the women's were concealed by
traditional veils. In the mosque women had to wear a *maghnae*, a
broad headdress that covered the hair, and a *rupush*, a long overcoat, or a chador. Not far from Parì sat a woman with a bowed
head; she seemed intent on staring at the floor. She wore a chador
that covered her entire body: such a garment was called a "veil by
constriction, not by conviction." All you could tell was that she was
short, but under that huge cloak she could conceal all other traits.

I followed Parì home for the condolence ritual. I couldn't
resist asking her whether she knew the identity of that woman.

"What—you didn't see? It's Fariba."

"Since when has she dressed like that?"

"She's been brainwashed by her sister. The sister was already a
mujahidin, and when she left prison she gradually indoctrinated

Fariba. Now Fariba prays constantly, fasts during Ramadan, attends religious meetings, and looks with disdain on all her old friends—"

"And on Javad?" I interrupted, unable to hold back the question.

"Yes, me, too, Shirin *joon*," said Javad, who had come up behind me. "She told me that she's *haram* to me—prohibited. A man prohibited from his own wife—have you ever heard of such a thing?" He tried to maintain his usual tone, but I could hear the tension in his voice.

Ali, who had just joined us, couldn't let the golden opportunity go by. "It's truly a gift from Allah, the fact that a released militant could save a nonbeliever from darkness and put her on a better path to serve the Iranian people. Perhaps it'll be good for you, Javad, to have a true Muslim at your side."

Pari gave her younger brother a disapproving look—this conversation wouldn't lead anywhere positive.

"A reactionary, old-fashioned wife isn't helpful to anyone. We fight all the time."

"Javad, you're truly unlucky," said Simin, in a sympathetic tone. "I thought that a marriage, and perhaps some children, would have given you a happier, more stable life. But instead . . ."

Ali tried to interrupt, but Javad cut him off. "Don't say a word or I'll punch you."

"Javad!"

"*Maman*, don't get involved. I'm not going to beat him up, but if he tries to tell me that what Fariba's doing is right, I won't be able to stop myself."

"For the love of God, Ali, leave your brother alone. No matter what you think, it's obvious that they don't have a happy marriage. I only want to worry about things relating to this family. I'm not interested in politics and I'm not interested in your fighting."

Parì couldn't get another word in. She hated to see her brothers argue—Alì and Javad, Javad and Abbas, and it had been a continuous battle ever since the Revolution. The stubbornness of the three of them made her and her mother miserable, and there was no way to get them to stop. When they began to fight, Parì didn't get involved and couldn't even watch; she sat on her bed and thought, over and over: please stop. At that moment she was repeating please stop, please stop in her head. Sometimes it worked.

"Darling, you're not that unlucky. Don't get worked up over what Alì thinks."

"I'm not angry at him, I'm angry at all these reactionaries who are brainwashing Fariba. To think that I, of all people, ended up with an extremist wife! I'm the cultural leader of my political organization and I'm ashamed to see her pray."

Alì rotated his head from side to side, as if to loosen his neck muscles. He didn't bother to repress his smile.

"Try to have a little patience, Javad, and remember that I will always do whatever I can to help you," said Simin.

"Thanks, though there's not much you can do when Fariba calls me a hypocrite and a traitor. And she doesn't even understand that she's the one who's betrayed our beliefs, our movement, our friends. I'm tired of fighting in my own house. I can't go home anymore."

Simin made a signal to her children to lower their voices. "I told you that a marriage won't begin well without a *nabat*."

12

The *Pagosha* Revolutionary

SINCE HER CHILDREN had grown up, Simin had done nothing but dream about, imagine, and prepare for their weddings. She didn't try to select their spouses, but she expected to be consulted and to approve of her future daughters-in-law. "*Mobarak bashe*," congratulations, she would tell her, with a sweet smile—and then she'd embrace the bride. She wouldn't interfere in the choice of the dowry, praising whatever glasses, serving trays, linens, and kitchenware the daughter's mother might choose. Well, perhaps not the kitchenware, that is, if they bothered to ask her—she could provide that herself, famous cook that she was. And she would have certainly prepared almond, pistachio, and apple pastries, to serve at the first nuptial ceremony. She imagined a grand reception in a garden like the one at the old house in Abbas Abad, with flowers everywhere. And she would have made sure to organize the intimate, family dinner, the one for the closest relatives, cooking everything herself.

She had for some time been copying her secret recipes into three small leather-bound notebooks, which she planned to give to the three daughters-in-law upon returning from their honeymoons. "It's all yours. Now you're the one responsible for taking care of my son."

Touran had her notebook, but Parì had inherited the other two. It was out of the question that Fariba, even when she was still close to Javad, might take part in such a tradition: good soldier that she was, she had little time for cooking.

Alì relieved Simin of her final fairy tale. He chose as his wife Mariam, the cousin of his mullah, a young girl barely sixteen years of age, utterly unprepared to become a wife. Simin resolved to give the girl the notebook of recipes as soon as she was a bit more experienced, but she never had the chance.

Alì had expressed his desire to have Khomeini himself read the *khotbeh-ye aghd*, the sermon delivered by the mullah at the wedding ceremony. The procurator general and the uncle of the bride interceded on behalf of their old friend and the ayatollah officiated over the ceremony in person.

For security reasons, however, attendance at the wedding had to be carefully supervised: only the parents of the couple and Mariam's uncle could participate.

"Even I can't go, can you believe that?" Parì said to me. "Maybe it's better this way. I wanted to see Alì's wedding, but not Ayatollah Khomeini."

In honor of the new regime, her brother had imposed a rule of absolute sobriety. There would be no additional ceremonies or parties, and certainly no lunches, to Simin's great displeasure. He granted her only the duty of organizing the *pagosha* party, in which the bride would be formally introduced to the groom's relatives and friends. Alì requested that there be a limited meal, because true revolutionaries hate waste and the ostentation of luxury. His mother complied by serving steamed rice with a few vegetables, yogurt, and a little meat.

*   *   *

WHEN I ARRIVED AT THE PARTY for Alì and Mariam, I found
the small apartment packed with guests. Parì greeted me right
away and took my coat. I began to hand her my foulard, but she
grabbed my wrist and whispered to me: "Please, don't take it off."
It was only then that I realized she was wearing one, too, tied
under her chin to cover her hair. We were obliged to wear them
in public, but usually took them off when we went into a private
home; only the most fanatical wore them at all times.

I readjusted my foulard. Parì shrugged. "I'm sorry," she said,
and took me by the arm into the living room. The larger pieces
of furniture had been cleared out for the occasion. At the center
of the room stood the old *korsì*, which had been cleaned and was
gleaming; on top of it Simin had laid out her modest refreshments.
Two rows of chairs were reserved for the men; on the opposite
side of the room there were others for the women. Almost all of
the ladies wore the chador, except those cousins of Alì who made
do with only the foulard. Seeing this I felt suffocated.

"I know what you're thinking," Parì said to me under her
breath. "Please, I beg you, just sit down and let it pass. As soon as
I can get free, we'll talk."

I backed myself into a quiet corner and wondered how long
I had to stay to avoid seeming rude. The men spoke animatedly.
Abbas and Javad hadn't shown up. The women sat in silence, staring at the floor. Though some dared to lean toward their neigh-
bor and whisper something in her ear.

Alì stood in the middle of the room, listening closely to the
words of his mullah. He still had the same short hair, and the
beard that was now long and ragged, covering his sunken cheeks.
There was a hardened expression on his face and his eyes were

serious. But still he was just playing at being a man—his narrow shoulders, soft hands, and the deferential, almost infantile manner in which he spoke to his mullah betrayed his eighteen years.

A large photograph of the wedding hung on the wall. It showed Ayatollah Khomeini reading the *khotbeh-ye aghd* while the couple stood in the background. The bride wore a plain, unpretentious dress.

I found her among her guests, seated apart, seemingly disoriented and embarrassed by the gathering. She had a round face and small heart-shaped lips that furrowed into a grimace as soon as someone started speaking to her. Two dimples formed on her cheeks whenever she smiled. Simin went over and gave her an affectionate pat on the cheek. From that simple gesture I could tell that she loved her young daughter-in-law, despite her meager culinary gifts.

Parì joined me an hour later. "Can you give me a hand with the entrees?"

I followed her into the kitchen. "I'm sorry for my lack of hospitality, but I can't stand that morgue anymore."

"Thanks for saving me."

Parì started to prepare the tea.

"See what my sister-in-law is doing to me? Of all the nice girls in Tehran, Alì had to take a wife from one of the most fanatical, ignorant families."

Parì called the revolutionaries "ridiculous" because she thought that they didn't know how to enjoy life. When, during the Revolution, I went out into the square and rallied for Khomeini, she made fun of me: "You're as ridiculous as all the rest of them!"

Parì had stayed faithful to her determination to keep away from politics. Javad had tried a few times to drag her to some of the meetings of the Tudeh, but she told him she could think of better ways to pass the time.

By this point, however, it had become clear that she wasn't being entirely straightforward—she had made a decision to avoid losing her brothers, to maintain what was left of her family. She was determined not to end up, like them, locked in a golden cage. Parì had different ambitions for her future. After getting her advanced degree in London, she took a job as a professor at the University of Tehran. In the mornings she taught, in her "chic and intellectual" manner; afternoons she worked in a small health care clinic in the suburbs. Most of her patients were unable to pay for her services, but she wouldn't trade for a nicer office in the city. "Why would I want to spend more time at the university? I'm there enough as it is," she said, shrugging her shoulders. She refused to listen whenever she was praised as good or generous.

In the living room they started singing the *salawat*, the song that praised Allah and the Prophet. Before the Revolution, it was only sung during times of bereavement, but since music and applause had become prohibited, it was used to celebrate happy occasions, too.

"What kind of *pagosha* is this?" Parì blurted out, with a smirk. "Feels more like a funeral. And now they're starting again with the revolutionary hymns. 'Oh Khomeini, you symbol of honor, you martyr for the cause!'" she sang, mockingly.

"Parì, you're impossible," I said, trying to suppress my laughter. "They might hear you and get offended. At the end of the day, you have to let everyone celebrate the way they want. Or do you think they should all do exactly as you do?"

"They can sing the *salawat* as much as they care to. I only want to be allowed to celebrate my own way. It's the revolutionaries who prevent me from behaving the way I'd like. As if it weren't enough that they were taking away my little brother."

Now I understood why she was so unhappy. "Did Alì find an apartment?"

"For the moment they're going to stay in a room at her family's house, until they find a small place for themselves."

"Can't they stay here?"

"*Maman* would love it—but Alì refuses. And you know why? Me. My behavior and my style of talking would offend poor Mariam. That's the reason."

There was embarrassed silence between us, which Parì tried to defuse by shrugging her shoulders in her characteristic way.

"You know what Alì did on the day of his wedding? He asked Saint Khomeini if he could name his firstborn son after him. What an insufferable toad."

"What did Khomeini say?"

"What do you think? He said yes, of course. 'I bless you, *inshallah.*'"

"What about your mother—what does she think of Mariam? It seems that she likes her."

"Yes, she says she's a good girl. Then again she's the granddaughter of the procurator and will surely help Alì along in his career. Already he's been nominated to be a judicial investigator," she explained, giving me a sidelong glance.

I almost jumped when I heard that. Here I was, despite my

experience, having to take a clerical job, while Alì, who had never even seen a law book, would be an investigator?

"Alì doesn't have the training. Since when can a judicial investigator not have a law degree?"

"Since the procurators don't need to have one either," said Parì, with impeccable logic.

13
Under Surveillance

ONE RING, two, three rings.

Parì ran to pick it up. "Hello? Hello?" Nothing. She put down the phone.

"Who was it?" Simin asked from the kitchen.

"No one."

"Again?"

Parì didn't even bother to respond. She picked up the telephone, dialed a number, then put it down.

"It's the second time today," she said, turning to me. "It's been going on for two months now. They call, a couple of times a day, and they don't say anything. It's enough to make you go crazy."

"A prankster?" I asked.

"I'm afraid not. *Maman* can't take it anymore. Yesterday she burst into tears on the telephone. When I came back from the clinic I found her with the phone still in her hand. The anxiety is killing her."

"What's wrong, Parì? You know you can tell me."

Parì let out a deep breath. She let herself slide down on the divan and hugged a silk cushion. Her lips trembled. She tried to hold back her tears. She had the same tense expression on her face as when they had arrested her brother. And the reason, I intuited, was the same, too.

"It's Javad, isn't it?" I asked. Ever since the shah had fled abroad, the alliance between the nationalists, communists, and Islamic groups had dissolved like snow in sunlight. And since Khomeini took power he had been rooting out, one by one, his former supporters, purging the enemies of Allah and of Iran. The members of the Tudeh were, in this phase, his main target.

"Yes. He says that the same thing happens at his house, and at Fariba's parents' house. It's a new form of wiretapping: they call you up, wait until someone picks up, and then hang up." The next call you make is automatically intercepted. "He told me that every time it happens I should call the operator, so that they tap the wrong call."

"Are you sure? You're not exaggerating?" I still wondered whether she was teasing me, her voice dropping lower and lower as we spoke.

"I thought so myself at first—that Javad, after his horrible experience, had become paranoid, that he felt himself constantly persecuted, as when the Savak was after him. But the telephone calls continued, and too often. And all of his old friends are being eliminated, one by one. They're either arrested or they vanish."

Parì couldn't go on. Tears fell down her cheeks and dampened the brown silk of the cushion. I sat next to her and embraced her. I'd never seen her so fragile.

"I'm sorry, Shirin, I just can't handle the stress anymore. To stay here and simply wait. . . . You know, I'm almost relieved when no one responds. When I hear the phone ring I always think that it'll be someone telling me that Javad has been arrested. It'll happen sooner or later." With the back of her hand she wiped away the last tears and sat up straight. "What do you think we should do?"

"Can't he turn himself in?" I hazarded. "All he did for the Tudeh was serve as cultural director. Maybe he'd get off easy. . . ." I knew that the new government, promising clemency, had ordered the members of the party to turn themselves over to the authorities immediately.

"No, he doesn't trust them. And this time, he's right. I don't want him to end up on the 'ramp of repentance.'"

Political prisoners were sent to a jail in Evin, north of Tehran. Before one reached the prison gate, there was a very steep incline; to taunt the counterrevolutionaries, the prison guards told them that the ramp would make them repent, even before they got to the prison. It became known as the "ramp of repentance."

"Besides, you know him," she continued. "He's not one for penitence. Even if he were sent to jail, he wouldn't rat on his fellow travelers and he wouldn't renounce his beliefs. Not even under torture. He'd prefer to die. He's already been close to death, with the Savak."

The Savak, an acronym for *Sazeman-e Ettela'at va Amniyat-e Kehvar*, the Organization of National Security and Information, was the secret police during the time of the shah. Their official mandate was to protect the country, but in fact they persecuted any political activist who opposed the monarchy. Their methods included electroshock therapy, beatings, and red-hot irons; sometimes they pulled out prisoners' fingernails. Horrific as this might seem, such tactics were not particularly novel—they were employed by secret police all over the world, long before the Savak, and the same atrocities are still committed to this day. But the Pasdaran were worse than the Savak. They were convinced that they were acting in the name of Islam and Allah—that they had been called to a higher duty and would be rewarded with eternal salvation. For this reason one couldn't appeal to their religious values: they represented a force of good that transcended such earthly concerns as misery, so they didn't hesitate to torture their prisoners with astonishing cruelty. They were also drawn by the bitter and inebriating seductions of power. The Savak, at least, always remained a strictly-defined military organization, in which every operative reported to his superior. The Pasdaran were like mad dogs unleashed by a single owner—Khomeini. And within the established hierarchy it was possible to create one's own personal reign of terror.

All this passed through my mind as Parì was talking, but I couldn't divulge my thoughts. Instead I asked,

"Has Javad thought of leaving town?"

"And go where? Tehran or somewhere else, it's all the same as far as he's concerned. The truth is that he doesn't want to abandon his sinking ship: the party. It's his foolish idealism again."

As Parì showed me to the door, she said, "Listen, everything I've told you—it has to stay between us, OK?"

I was offended: how could she doubt my loyalty? This, too, was from the Pasdaran's influence: they had made friends and family members suspicious of each other.

JAVAD SLIPPED AWAY from his apartment in secrecy, resigning himself to a clandestine existence. He didn't take any books or clothing with him: he wanted to give the impression that he'd return soon. Fariba moved back to her parents' house, promising that she would join him soon, but her devotion to her husband had already vanished—if it had even been there to begin with. Much later, Parì told me the truth about their marriage:

the Tudeh—to which they both belonged at the time—had asked them to wed, so that they could run a clandestine cell together. As husband and wife, they'd be less suspicious.

Two days after he fled, the Pasdaran visited Simin's house. They barged in and turned the apartment upside down in search of clues to his whereabouts. They came back the following day, and the one after that, searching in the same places each time.

"What idiots!" said Parì, exasperated. "What do they think, that my brother is hiding in the credenza?" But as long as they kept searching, she could be sure that Javad was free.

He never sent news of himself, not wanting to endanger his mother and sister. When he became overwhelmed by nostalgia, he reappeared, without any advance notice. A few weeks earlier he had grown a shaggy beard so that he'd blend in with the Ayatollah's loyalists.

"See what I have to do to come be with you?" he said, hugging them.

He lived like this for a full year, moving from one hiding spot to another, always more alone. His marriage to Fariba was over. When finally it seemed that the waters had calmed, he returned to his mother's house. But the telephone calls started again soon after, the implacable soundtrack to a drama whose ending had already been written.

14
Twenty Years in a Single Night

SIMIN AND PARÌ begged me to come right away to their house for a legal consultation. I went there immediately, alarmed by the tone of their message.

"Shirin *joon*, it's so nice of you to come," said Simin when she greeted me. "God bless you." The door had opened before I even rang the bell. They sat me down in the living room, where three trays filled with various types of pastries awaited me. Parì appeared with the tea.

"As you see, *maman* has outdone herself," she said, greeting me. "Today you're a special guest." Her casual tone reassured me: whatever it was couldn't be too serious.

"Shirin is always a special guest," Simin said.

"Actually what happened is that *maman* couldn't sit still," said Parì, sighing. "All afternoon she's been kneading and baking away. That's what she always does when she's nervous: cook. After all that Javad has put us through, now the cupboards are bursting full."

"When you're a mother you'll understand," snapped Simin.

"So what's going on?" I asked, to put an end to the squabbling.

"This time it's Abbas. Even my quiet older brother is causing headaches, can you believe it? As you know, not long before the Revolution, he followed Borna and Arya to America. He was hoping he'd return, along with his shah, but now—well, anyway, he's going to stay in America. The problem is his apartment. They want to seize it." Parì handed me a letter.

After the Islamic Revolution, a law was passed that gave the state the right to claim all property belonging to Iranian citizens who had been abroad for more than a year. Property belonging to citizens who were being sought by the state or had already been sentenced to prison was confiscated and appropriated immediately; in other cases the measure was temporary. When the person returned to the country, he could reclaim possession of his property, as long as he covered the enormous costs of "management." The law was intended to discourage expatriation, but it wasn't effective: almost four million Iranians fled the country, abandoning their homes and their possessions, even their loved ones. The revolutionaries became noticeably wealthier, and purchased real estate that was selling at half its value. Owners returned to find their apartments having already been sold, and the modest revenue from the sale would barely cover the "management" fees.

At the time I didn't know much about this practice. I began to read the document that Parì had handed to me. It said that Abbas had to appear within a week, otherwise the state would be forced to take the necessary measures, etcetera. The deadline had already passed.

"Is there anything we can do?" Simin asked anxiously.

"I'm sorry, but I don't think so. I need to study the law and find out if there is any precedent for this. Try not to worry," I reassured her. "Tomorrow I'll talk with a former colleague of mine and I'll let you know if there's any way out of this."

"Thanks, we're indebted to you. We decided not to tell Abbas. *Maman* worries that he'll decide to return and try to solve things his own way," said Parì, quietly.

"Don't worry, it'll be OK," I replied, displaying a certainty that I didn't really feel.

ABBAS HAD LEFT ON A CLEAR WINTER morning many months earlier. It was during the time of the demonstrations and the strikes; the news reports were getting more alarming by the day, and the shah seemed to be on the verge of fleeing, but nothing in the world would stop Touran from making her annual visit to her children. They packed a single, small piece of luggage: it wasn't cold in Los Angeles and they didn't need much clothing. Anything else they needed they could find at their children's house.

Abbas had gotten in line at the airport check-in, while Touran took a seat nearby and waited. During the period in which they'd been planning the trip, Abbas briefly thought about not joining her and staying behind to fight the hordes of madmen who wanted to drive out the shah. Then he caught sight of his wife, falling asleep in front of the television. She lay in a fetal position, her knees pressed to her chest. Her face, lit by the glow of the screen, was waxen and hollow, and she seemed even more worried than usual. On her shoulders her long black hair showed the first streaks of gray. But she still seemed beautiful to him, as when in childhood he spied on her doing the laundry in the garden.

She had been diagnosed with a late-stage breast tumor. She had taken the news of her illness with a sense of resignation, almost serenity. She put herself in the hands of God, as she always had. She underwent the operation with confidence. Abbas had taken her to the hospital, caressing her thin fingers and speaking to her until the doctors came to take her away.

When they returned to Iran, she would begin the first cycles of chemotherapy, which would make her full, silky hair begin to fall out. Abbas was inconsolable. How could he live without Touran? He had lost Iran, the shah, and his job, but that was nothing compared to losing her, his one source of stability, the person he held more precious than anything else.

He refused to deprive Touran of seeing Borna and Arya, and couldn't let her go to America alone. They would go together as a family, perhaps for the last time.

THE NIGHT AFTER OUR MEETING I got a call from Parì.

"Shirin, forget about trying to figure out about the apartment. A friend of mine just told me that the property seizure is set for tomorrow. We got there too late. If only the doorman had warned us! We found the envelope in the middle of a bunch of bills."

"I'm really sorry. I imagine that must have been terrible news for Abbas."

"We still haven't told him," said Parì. "The damage is already done. I'd rather tell him when everything is over. Tonight *maman* and I are going to pick up his most precious belongings and store them in an old garage. Then we'll decide what to do about them." There was exhaustion in her voice.

I was fairly depressed by the time I got off the phone with her. I looked around me with an uneasy sensation: the couch, the armchairs, the embroidered cushions, the slightly-worn rug, the large vase in which I'd arranged fresh flowers, the forms and the small imperfections of the furnishings that I knew by heart. I'd always believed that all of this was completely, absolutely mine. A doorman's neglectfulness was enough to cause Abbas to lose everything he had built over a lifetime, the tangible markers of his passage through time and the things that he loved. Strangers would soon move into his home, redecorate the rooms, perhaps even knock down a wall or two, and he couldn't do anything about it. I felt as if my home had been violated as well.

All night I dreamed of government agents searching my apartment.

That same night, without the help of even a glimmer of moonlight, Simin and Parì went to Abbas's house. It looked as if he had been gone for years. It was dark, dank, and full of dust; it was as if rubble had fallen from the ceiling. Who knows if Abbas would have ever wanted to step foot again in a house that had survived the Revolution and, in its degradation, was a testimony to the fall of the shah.

"Don't cry, *Maman*, I beg you," said Parì when they entered. "Now's not the time. We should hurry." She turned on the light and walked into the center of the living room, trying not to cough as she inhaled the heavy air.

"I can't worry about your brothers so much anymore, Parì. It's not right that a weak mother should suffer this way. Why did God want this for me?" This lamentation for her sons had become a common refrain, even though she would always greet them with open arms when they came to see her.

"Don't bring God into this, please, or I'm really going to get mad," said Parì, lifting a low wooden table off the rug. "God has nothing to do with this. We're here, you and me, and if you don't want to give me a hand it'd be best if you just leave."

With a glance to her mother—who was still standing in the doorway, debating whether to leave everything behind and run away from the pain, or recover whatever was left—Parì began to roll up the rug that covered the entire living room floor. Finally Simin's sense of duty, and her inability to stand by with her hands in her pockets, prevailed. She loosened the foulard from around her head and knelt beside her daughter, her strong hands grabbing the fringe of the expensive rug. The carpet, which originally had belonged to her grandmother, was still in excellent condition—they could get a good price for it.

"Thank you," said Parì, though now it was she who was on the verge of giving up.

When they finished with the rug, they began to push the furniture toward the door.

"Not that one, even though it's held up," said Simin, pointing to a pale, slightly faded wooden chest of drawers. Parì opened the first drawer, which was crammed full of papers. "Not worth a penny," she said, nodding in agreement, and went into the bedroom to evaluate the condition of the other things.

Simin showed a surprising amount of energy and determination: they had little time and her sense of resolve proved critical. She went through each room and inspected the furniture, telling Parì what to abandon—which was really very little since Abbas's house had been beautifully furnished. Parì, meanwhile, quickly went through the smallest objects, especially in the office and in the bedroom, looking for anything of value, a jewel or even a silver fitting from the desk. They'd drag the furniture toward the door, then move on to the next room.

They went on like this for a few hours. At dawn, as planned, one of their cousins showed up to help them move the furniture in his van. They were finished at seven. They had only needed a single night to erase every trace of Abbas from the house where he had lived for twenty years.

15

From Dates to the United Nations in a Single Fax

DONALD RUMSFELD SHOOK Saddam Hussein's hand and laughed for the television cameras. I couldn't believe my eyes. I stared at the screen, almost expecting that the strength of my incredulity would make the image disappear. But the BBC news program had already moved on to a much more urgent story, the Los Angeles Olympics. It was like they didn't realize they'd just announced the end of the world. Of our world, at least. We were done for.

"Maliheh," I asked my sister, "do you get CNN? Can we watch the news again?"

"Hold on, let me try to find the right channel."

That year we'd decided to take a brief trip to my sister's villa on the Caspian Sea. After the beginning of the war with Iraq in 1980, food had been rationed and essential goods were in short supply. It was easier to find them there near the sea, because we could supplement our rations with goods purchased on the black market, which was booming thanks to access to the ports and contraband smuggled in from Turkey.

And there were benefits to living in a calmer place. The Iraqi invasion had given the government a perfect pretext to close ranks and govern in the names of Allah, Khomeini, and Iran. These efforts had yielded an aggressive flurry of patriotism and an even more ferocious and radical persecution of political dissidents, who were accused of being spies sent by the Great Satan, the United States, and by the Little Satan, Iraq. Every word needed to be carefully chosen to avoid denunciation and suspicion, and everyone had to praise the Revolution and the war without hesitation.

Every day the national television stations and newspapers reported news of courageous conquests, brave deeds, and heroic resistance to the enemy. The fallen were honored as *shahid*, martyrs for Allah; their families could be assured that they had earned places in paradise. And they emphasized that our losses were infinitely less than those of our enemies, those thousands of Iraqis who were exterminated every day by our blessed military.

"If these numbers were right, the Iraqi people would have gone extinct a long time ago," said my husband, as he angrily turned the pages of the newspaper.

The only reliable news came from abroad, but it was becoming increasingly difficult to access. In Iran it was forbidden to have a satellite dish or watch foreign television programs. Even today, the regime's agents will burst into people's homes and confiscate illegal antennae. Besides the legal problems this creates for the tenant, the building owners must also pay enormous fines. But in the villa on the Caspian Sea, unpestered by state officials, my sister had an antenna and we could get a signal from most international channels. When we finally found a news report that hadn't been manufactured by the regime, we felt an elation that I'd never forget. But soon we realized how critical the situation was for Iran—far worse than what we had imagined—and the news reports became a daily torture.

That day our worst fears had been confirmed: the United States, our historic and meddlesome ally of thirty years, was supporting Iraq. Donald Rumsfeld had been asked by Ronald Reagan to demonstrate to the entire world how isolated Iran had become.

The initial impact was devastating. But soon it had the opposite effect, turning those who opposed the regime into supporters. That same video was broadcast a few days later on national television as a form of propaganda, leaving a terrible impression in the eyes and minds of all Iranians: Satan really was against us after all. This feeling of being ostracized, hunted by a jackal and its rich, heavily-armed friends, helped to restore our solemn and unconditional support of the Islamic Republic.

Men both young and old enlisted, eager to fill the ranks of an army that had been decimated—first by the postrevolutionary purges, then by the number of those who had been lost in the war. The poor, who were promised a pension for them and their families, were the most likely to throw themselves into the melee. Their lives were worth very little to them. Even Ali had set off for battle, motivated by political furor and his love for Khomeini. He had taken Mariam and Ruhollah with him, settling first in Ahvaz, the capital of Khuzestan Province. This region, which lay on the border of Iraq, had been invaded by Saddam Hussein in an attempt to bring the Iranian economy to its knees—the nation's largest oil wells and the great Abadan refinery were located there. Iraq counted on winning the support of the local population, which was made up of various ethnic minorities, including three million Arabs who had endured a long history of persecution. Instead the Iranians stayed united, fighting in the streets with the courage of lions. In the few letters he was able to send, Ali wrote about how proud he was to fight alongside such fearless compatriots.

Javad, on the other hand, had left Tehran. He feared a new police crackdown on dissidents, and instead returned to Rasht.

Iraq's military superiority was crushing: Saddam Hussein didn't hesitate to employ chemical warfare, or bomb cities— first in the north and then Tehran itself, the flaming trails of the falling missiles illuminating the night sky. It was impossible to sleep because of the distant—or terrifyingly close—explosions, and the constant ringing of alarms. We raced to improvised public air-raid shelters, which weren't necessarily any safer but at least we felt less alone. The mind sought out the whistling of the bombs; we followed them at night as we lay there awake, with our eyes closed, taking a deep breath of relief whenever they landed in a different neighborhood. We'd survived once again.

Exhausted by fear and too many sleepless nights, I returned with my parents to Maliheh's place, on the Caspian Sea. We listened, sunk in our chairs, to the sound of the same bombs now transmitted on television. Then we ran to call friends and relatives in the attacked areas to find out if they were OK. We hadn't been able to leave behind our uneasiness and stress, and we felt a gnawing sense of guilt for having extricated ourselves from what otherwise might have been a very different fate.

It was my father who finally said what none of us dared to. "I'm going back today. Back to Tehran." We turned to him, terrified. We knew that sooner or later the moment would come when we'd have to return, but none of us would have ever had the courage to declare it openly, in front of everyone.

"I want to go back to my house," he continued. "If anyone wants to come with me, get your things ready. Whoever wants to remain here, please, finish the rest of your breakfast."

My sister interrupted. "Maybe we should wait a few more days. The danger hasn't passed."

"My dear Maliheh, you can't escape fate. Does everyone who lives in Tehran have a villa where they can run to and hide?"

She stared at him uncomprehendingly.

"Everything that they suffer, we will suffer, too," my father said.

I feared for my children's safety—I wouldn't want to subject them to such an imprudent plan—but there was no way I would let my parents go back to Tehran alone. So I decided to return to the life of bombardments and wreckage. I felt slightly reckless but at the same time I'd finally freed myself from that subtle, gnawing sense of guilt.

As soon as we got home I made dinner for my children and put them to bed. Then I listened to the messages on my voice mail. Most of them had been left by friends asking whether we were OK. We had informed the fewest number of people possible about our departure, fearing that the apartment might be attacked by thieves entering like jackals to steal what little remained of our ruined lives.

Pari was one of the few people who knew about our absence. So I was surprised to have three messages from her. She begged me, in an agitated tone, to call her back as soon as possible. I did, even though by now it was already past midnight. Her voice was the same as it had been on the messages: anxious, frantic even.

"I have to see you immediately, Shirin *joon*," she said. "It's urgent."

It was clear that we couldn't speak freely on the telephone, so we made an appointment to meet at ten o'clock the next morning at my house. Parì arrived fifteen minutes early. She seemed shaken; I had hardly opened the door and invited her in when she began to talk.

"They arrested Javad," she blurted out, and her body went limp—emptied of the news that she had bottled up for days.

"What happened?"

"We don't know anything. They've already had him for a few weeks. The police attacked the party's central location: two are dead and the others are in prison. Javad is with them."

"Where have they put him?"

Parì shrugged. "We don't know."

"How'd you find out?"

"One of his friends. He wasn't at Rasht during the raid so he got away. When he saw that the apartment where they had lived had been destroyed, he escaped for Pakistan—for Baluchistan. He called me as soon as the UN accepted him in its program to protect political refugees." Parì nervously passed her hand through her hair.

"And Fariba," I ventured, "does she know?"

"Her? She hasn't been around for a long time. She says she doesn't want to have anything to do with a nonbeliever. You should hear how scornfully she says my brother's name. Poor Javad." Her voice softened. "He's been so unhappy these past few years: his marriage over, no children, being forced to go into hiding, always on the run . . . but I can't bear to imagine what might happen to him in jail." She had tears in her eyes. She was thinking, like me, about how her brother had declined during his first imprisonment. "Now we're at war. It'll be even worse. Much worse."

"What do you think we should do?" I asked Parì.

"Shirin *joon*, you stood beside me the other time. I'm here to ask you to help me again. Do you know any judges who might be willing to see me and at least tell me where Javad is? You know that I wouldn't involve you if I had any other options."

"Most of the judges that I know have been dismissed, like me. Those now in charge obey every order and have no power, especially when it comes to political detainees." I felt extremely uncomfortable. I stood up and walked nervously into the kitchen, trying to figure out what to do.

"So you're telling me there's nothing?" she asked.

"Nothing that involves the judges, no," I responded bitterly. "What about Alì? Might he be willing to help you this time?" I added, knowing the answer.

"No, Alì hates Javad and won't raise a finger. In fact, after the rise of Khomeini, Alì developed a hatred for practically everybody who wasn't on his side. He stopped speaking with Javad and refuses even to mention Abbas by name. He says that he's ashamed to have a brother who served as a general."

Once again I found myself thinking of everything that Abbas—despite his blind loyalty to the shah, and even his limited intelligence—had done for his brothers. He had raised them both, made them do their studies and deprived himself of so much to take care of them. Now they both looked upon him with hatred, disowning him.

We sat in silence for several minutes. My mind was working feverishly but it was closed off, a room without doors; I had no answers. Then Parì exclaimed: "Wait—can't you contact international agencies—Amnesty International, for example, or Human Rights Watch? What do you think?"

I remembered that the United Nations Commission on Human Rights had recently sent a "special permanent representative" to Iran. His name was Reynaldo Galindo Pohl. In the past years the human rights violations reported in Iran had been so egregious that the United Nations had asked one of their own representatives to observe the situation firsthand. Naturally once he had reported what he had seen, the Iranian government had denounced him and forbade him from entering the country again.

"I'll write to Amnesty, the UN's Reynaldo Galindo Pohl, the UN Commission on Human Rights, Human Rights Watch, and every other organization I can think of," I said to Parì. "I'll tell them what's happened to Javad."

She seemed relieved. I took a piece of paper and a pen from my office desk and began to write in Farsi, while Parì translated into English. After having corrected and rewritten the letter several times, I signed it and we decided to send it by post the next day. Before putting it in an envelope, we reread it again, to make certain that we hadn't forgotten anything. I had written that I knew Javad well and that he had nothing to do with the war; he was the director of cultural affairs for his party and he had been arrested for his political beliefs. He had been denied every basic human right granted to prisoners, including the right to consult with a lawyer, and the right to see his family.

After the letter was finished I prepared us a pot of tea. The work had exhausted us but we couldn't rest; we kept talking about various unrelated matters, in a pathetic effort to recover some sense of normalcy. Parì even smiled once or twice and the tension of keeping up appearances lifted until, as she raised her cup, she said, "Shirin, at the post office they will see who the letters are addressed to and they won't send them. Especially when they see who's sending them. It's pointless. There's no way out."

Unfortunately she was right. In Iran the level of oppression had never been so high; using national security and the war with Iraq as a pretext, the state monitored the telephone lines and the mail. Extreme measures weren't taken against everyone, of course, but those whom the regime suspected of being in contact with international organizations were under close surveillance. I was one of those people. On a number of occasions I had not received letters or packages that had been sent through the postal system by friends who had assured me they had sent them. I couldn't be certain that the state censors had intercepted my mail, but my letters for Javad ran the risk of not being delivered.

"Maybe it would be better to telephone," said Parì.

"No," I said. "Even if I were to call from a phone booth it'd be useless. The charges need to be written on paper. However . . ."

"However?" asked Parì anxiously.

"If we could get access to a fax machine—that might be a solution."

A ponderous silence again filled the room. Finally Parì looked up.

"Abbas had an old friend in Tehran. His name is Farid. He has a small exportation business, in dates. He has no interest in politics and his telephone line won't be tapped."

"If he has no interest in politics," I said, "he won't risk his business for us."

"But his son would!" Parì said enthusiastically.

"What?"

"Farid has a son with leftist sympathies. He's one of my students, I know him well. He'd do anything to expose the regime's crimes."

I thought about it for a minute. She might be on to something.

"The important thing is that his father doesn't find out about any of this," I said. We finally had found a solution.

We took the letters out of the envelopes, and on a slip of paper I wrote the fax numbers. I stuffed everything into a new envelope. That night she would contact her student and ask for his help.

I prepared some more tea. As soon as I carried the cups back to the table, Parì said, "Shame on you, Shirin! What about lunch? You have a guest, you know. I'm practically dying of starvation."

Now that there was hope for Javad, she'd recovered her irreverence.

"You got here at dawn," I replied. "I haven't had time to prepare anything. Look, so you don't die of hunger, I'll order some *chelow kebab.*"

"Good, have it delivered," Parì said, smiling. "For once it won't be ruined by your obsession with saffron."

46

The Doctor's Justice

JAVAD'S STORY WAS NOT an exceptional one in Khomeini's Iran. I received a sad reminder of this one morning not long after I heard the news of his arrest. My mother called me, overcome with anxiety; without even bothering to say hello, she said: "Shirin, they arrested the doctor."

The "doctor," as we called him, was my uncle. My grandfather had died prematurely and my father, at a very young age, was forced to take care of his mother and little brother—which he did, despite having to make many sacrifices. With his help, my uncle studied medicine in Europe, specializing in ophthalmology. He had gone on to become one of the most esteemed doctors in all of Iran. Now, in his sixties, he had left behind his university chair, and private practice, and lived in peace with his family. I didn't see how he could have irritated the regime.

"*Maman*, are you sure? What happened?"

"I don't know exactly," she said breathlessly. "They called this morning. He has been accused of having participated in a coup d'état."

"But that's ridiculous. How could they think that an old and respectable doctor is plotting against the regime?"

It had to be a mistake. One of many, unfortunately. The government was in a perpetual state of alert, especially since the outbreak of the war, and any type of behavior could be subject to misinterpretation. The allegation that someone was participating in a coup d'état was the most common outcome: when in doubt, the state saddled every criminal, whether guilty or simply suspected, with this gratuitous accusation. The slightest suspicion, unsupported by any evidence, was enough to arrest an innocent man, keep him in jail for months, torture him to obtain improbable confessions, and execute him. Then there were those cases in which the government would change its mind and plead "miscarriage of justice." The government had already done this numerous times, pardoning itself for unjust executions and celebrating the victims as martyrs—as if they had chosen to die to satiate the paranoia of the government. The victim's family received a pension equal to that received by families who had lost a son in war.

My uncle had surely been framed by this perverse and unpredictable mechanism. We had to intervene right away to determine the specifics of the case and exculpate him. That is, if we weren't already too late.

"What does *baba* say?" I asked.

"He doesn't know yet, I haven't had the courage to tell him. That's why I called you, Shirin. I'd prefer if you tell him. You know how to calm him down." My mother was pleading now. My father had recently suffered a heart attack and the news that his brother was in danger might be too much for him to bear.

"OK, I'll come over now."

I showed up at my parents' house at lunchtime. I pretended that I'd decided to stop in by chance. After lunch my father tended to take a nap, so I hoped I could speak with my mother alone. I signaled to her not to say anything and we waited for him to retire.

It was the most difficult lunch of my life: my father kept talking about things that now seemed ridiculous—the scarce rations, the empty gas pumps, the curfews—while my mind wandered. I tried to keep the conversation going but it felt as if someone else were speaking for me. I felt a terrible pang of guilt at the thought that I was, in some way, lying to my father.

As soon as we were alone, my mother told me that she'd received a dozen phone calls. Friends and relatives had heard about the arrest and they'd called to find out what had happened, and show their solidarity; to keep this from *baba* she was forced toward vagueness with them and finally to end the conversations abruptly. Inevitably my father would figure out what had happened, in some horrible manner, so she wanted to tell him as soon as possible.

When he came out after his nap, I joined him in the living room with a steaming cup of tea. I sat in front of him and did a brief mental prayer. The moment had arrived.

"Have you heard, *Baba*?" I said, staring at him closely. "They've been arresting more and more people. The regime has no scruples about going after innocents. Fortunately they're freed as soon as the judges realize the error. In fact, strong policies have now been put in place to ensure that the victims of these injustices get released."

My father stared at me in surprise. He'd never heard me use such a conciliatory tone when talking about the regime.

"It might not be of much consolation to those poor men, but at least they avoid a worse alternative." He continued to watch me, trying to figure out why I'd brought this up.

"Yes, exactly, I agree." I gathered my courage. "Well, *Baba*, you see, the doctor has ended up as one of those innocents."

He went pale. He put down the cup of tea and was silent for a few seconds. I didn't want to leave him alone with his thoughts so I started talking again.

"*Baba*, don't you see? It'll be easy to prove that he's not guilty. I'm going to handle it. All I have to do—"

Gently, he cut me off. "Shirin, it's fine, don't worry about me. I'm just amazed at what an ugly country we live in, where an old professor can't enjoy his pension in peace. What will the next generation ever do to fix this situation?"

"Take care of their uncles, no?" I said, trying to make light of the situation. But my voice was shaky, and my smile was forced. My father shook his head. He rested his hand on my shoulder and said, "Thank you. I'm glad that you'll handle it."

I went home immediately so that I could contact the human rights organizations. The date seller's fax machine functioned splendidly. Two days later I telephoned my aunt to find out what she'd heard. With the help of some connections she had been able to visit her husband in prison. The meeting had been rushed, and a guard hovered around them for at least ten minutes. The uncle was doing all right—emaciated but not discouraged. He explained why he was arrested. The brother of a childhood friend was the leader of an organization of political dissidents, and he had just been captured by the Pasdaran. In this man's address book they had found my uncle's telephone number; naturally he was deemed a suspect and arrested, along with everyone else whose name was listed. In a different context I might have laughed at the absurdity of the situation, but now I became filled with rage at this blatant violation of human rights, the precariousness in which we all found ourselves, and the realization of how far our judicial system had fallen.

Fortunately my uncle was certain that he would be released soon. Back at home we all took a deep breath and waited optimistically for new developments. But the days turned into months and nothing happened. We started to worry and soon slipped into a state in which we began to expect the worst. Which came soon enough.

One afternoon, a distant cousin stopped by my parents' house and asked to speak privately with my father. My father insisted, however, that I be present. "I keep no secrets from Shirin. Anything you say to me you can say to her." Not for the first time did I feel grateful to have him as my father. He had raised all his children as equals, and had taught me to assert my rights as a woman and how to refuse to accept discrimination. Though there had never been true equality between genders in Iran, our house was different. My father insisted upon equality, to a much greater extent than our mother, a traditional woman who often denied herself rights that she should have aspired to have.

"One of my closest friends has a son who is a Pasdar," began my cousin. "He works at Evin prison. He knew that the doctor was a prisoner there so he paid attention whenever his name came up in conversation. He's just learned that the doctor is on the list of those condemned to death. His execution is imminent."

My father, turning pale, collapsed into his chair. He was breathing heavily. I ran to get the portable oxygen tank and returned to his side, holding his hand. I tried desperately to think of some way to calm him down, but nothing came to mind. I was as stunned as he was.

"My friend's son knows the president of the tribunal," the cousin said, once my father recovered a bit. "He could put you in touch with him. All you need to do is bribe him, and the problem will be solved."

We knew all about the depravity of the tribunals. Tips and bribes were commonplace. A number of judges had been forced to resign because of corruption scandals. On this occasion, of course, this fact didn't make me indignant but brought a measure of joy: there was hope for my uncle.

"I'll pay whatever they want," said my father, the relief evident on his face.

A week later we were invited to Evin to see the doctor. Evidently Iran's "justice system" was functioning fine, as long as you knew who to pay. My father asked me to accompany him because he feared that he wouldn't be able to control his emotions—but as it turned out, this wasn't necessary. The day before the visit the doorbell at my parents' home rang. My mother raced to the door, yelling with joy: "The doctor's here! They've freed him, they've freed him!" My father and I watched her incredulously. We looked up, worried that it was a bad joke.

But there, at the door, was the doctor. Thin and pallid, sure, a little hunched over, and older than I remembered him, but it was him all right, in flesh and blood. He embraced us, smiling. My mother went off to call her family, while I prepared tea for everyone. Like my father and me, the doctor loved tea, and it was clear how much he missed it in prison.

When we'd sat again in the living room, my uncle explained why he had been released.

"At Evin there's a small hospital for the prisoners. When they discovered that I was a doctor they asked me to treat those who needed eye surgery. At first I wanted to refuse—the idea of collaborating with the Pasdaran horrified me—but then I realized that I could alleviate the suffering of the prisoners. I had nothing else to do, after all, and I wanted to make myself useful, to make my days count. Thus my career as a prison hospital surgeon was underway. There was only one other ophthalmologist so we took turns operating, assisting, and bandaging. I'd never worked so hard in my life."

Despite his emaciated frame, my uncle seemed to be in good spirits. My father's expression calmed with every word he spoke.

"Why were there so many people with eye problems? Was there some kind of epidemic?" I asked.

"Worse than an epidemic, my dear. They'd been tortured, you see. This gives a shock to the nervous system that causes the veins in the heart, kidneys, and eyes to burst. If the hemorrhaging isn't treated immediately the patient can go blind."

My mother broke in, impatiently: "Save that for later. Tell us about how you were released."

"Pure luck. While I was working at the hospital the head physician happened to stop by the facility and he recognized me. He had been a student of mine at the university and has since enjoyed a good career, helped along the way by his father-in-law, a mullah in Khomeini's circle. As soon as he heard my story he offered to help. He spoke with the president of the tribunal, and in less than two days he'd secured my release. The next morning he took me to sign several release forms." He smiled. "I didn't even have time to call you before I left."

There wasn't much to be proud of in the way that justice had been administered, I thought bitterly. My grandmother was right when she said that if you live long enough, you will one day see

things that once seemed impossible. As a child I had only understood the literal significance of this ancient Persian proverb, but
as an adult I intuited what it actually meant: the experience that
we accumulate day by day causes us to know and accept strange,
even incomprehensible realities—like that of a man arrested
by mistake, spared from execution by a bribe, and released by a
stroke of luck.

17
The Visit to Evin

As my family and I were trying to rescue the doctor, the letters that I'd sent for Javad started to work. One day Parì received a message on her voice mail that informed her of the date and hour in which she could visit the prisoner. It was a terse, unadorned message, but it gave her and her mother hope.

The day before the visit, Simin went to the bazaar and bought pounds of fresh fruit: apples, figs, and grapes with which she intended to pamper Javad as when he was a boy. Because of the rationing and the war, this gift cost a small fortune, but when it came to her children, it was worth it.

That morning she took great care with her dress, despite having already decided to wear a chador: it seemed important to ingratiate herself with the guards and demonstrate to them that she was the irreproachable mother of a son who was an honest man, despite the charges against him.

Parì observed these preparations in silence, because she didn't want her mother to hear, in her voice and in her words, what she truly felt: pity. Pity for herself for having chased after her stubborn brothers for years; for Javad and the hellish life to which he had been condemned; for Alì and Abbas and their silent rancor; but above all for Simin, who was as emotional as a little girl at the prospect of finally seeing one of her sons again. The last years had broken her heart: Abbas was stuck in America and might never return; Alì had chosen to move to the front and now didn't even bother to write home; Javad was unreachable, first because he was in hiding, now because he was in prison. Without them and without the grandchildren, she was a solitary woman and, worse, feeling like a useless mother. But the fighting and the tensions weighed more heavily on her than the nostalgia for better days. The sons were so rigid in their positions. It was as if they weren't brothers anymore. They didn't ask for news about each other's lives and shouted insults from afar; when they were in Tehran simultaneously, you could only see one at a time. The rowdy lunches at the old house in Abbas Abad were a distant memory.

LIKE PRISONERS, SIMIN AND PARÌ had to walk up the ramp of repentance. Parì wondered whether, when Javad was here, he had regretted, if only for a split second, some of the choices he'd made. She doubted it—he wasn't one for second thoughts. He and the others would have done the same thing no matter what the cost.

At the entrance the guards stopped them and grabbed the bags out of Simin's hands.

"There are no picnics here, grandmother," scoffed one of the guards. Despite his beard, he couldn't have been more than eighteen years old.

"It's only fruit," she responded, looking desolately at her two bags in the hands of the boy. "I brought it for my son."

"Sorry, grandma. This is now state property. Don't you know that prisoners can't receive gifts? They're not honored dignitaries. They're traitors."

"Forget about it, mom, let's not make a fuss," Parì begged her, putting her arm around her. She worried that her mother might snap at the insolent boy. But in fact she seemed on the edge of tears.

"You want to see your son or not?" he said, piling on, enjoying her pain.

"Come on." Parì went forward, gently taking her mother by the hand. Both lowered their heads, defeated, as they entered.

They were early; the previous visiting hours hadn't yet ended. They stood waiting for ten minutes, staring at the filthy walls, without saying a word. Then a guard ordered them to enter the visiting room; the earlier group was just leaving, relatives bending to hear one final detail before the gray curtain lowered completely and the prisoners disappeared from the other side of the glass. It was a dark room, four meters wide by twenty meters long; in the middle there was a wall, the upper half of which was a pane of glass, and on either side there were booths less than a meter wide, which were separated by thin partitions.

When the gray curtain rose again, Simin saw her son on the other side of the glass. She picked up the telephone in the booth and began to cry into the receiver. Parì went next; every so often she rested the phone gently on her shoulder but never broke eye contact with Javad. She wondered again whether he suffered at seeing the grief he'd inflicted upon them, if it caused him even a sliver of regret. But Parì was surprised to realize that she didn't nurture any resentment toward her obstinate brother. She only felt the urgency of imprinting in her memory his face, eyes, hair, and that easygoing smile that somehow still lingered on his lips.

Visits lasted just a few minutes: the detainees on their side of the wall, their relatives on the other—physical contact was not allowed. You couldn't even see them well: through the grimy glass Javad seemed somewhat out of focus. This much was clear, however: he had lost at least ten kilograms and much of his hair. A dirty beard covered his chin and cheeks, making even more prominent the darkness of his mouth. At the sight of his sister's insistent gaze, Javad smiled warmly.

"Hey, little sister," he whispered into the receiver, interrupting Simin's sobbing. The voice came across metallic and distorted through the divider. They had even stolen his voice from him, thought Parì.

"Write a letter of apology, ask for forgiveness, I beg you," Simin said with renewed vigor, heartened by her son's first affectionate words.

Javad didn't respond, only slightly shook his head, as if her pleading had nothing to do with him.

When his mother's prayers rose to a single, monotonous lament that flowed without interruption from one side of the wall to the other, he finally said, "Parì, maybe you can explain to *maman* why I can't."

"Javad, Javad, think of your youth. You still have a whole life ahead of you, you can be happy again. Look how your marriage ended up. What's made you so stubborn?"

"If you're just here to chastise me, then you shouldn't have bothered to come at all," he replied, losing his patience. "I have no intention of disowning my ideas. How could I face my peers? The party bosses are old, but even they resist torture. Should I give up after just a few months in prison?"

Parì exhaled uneasily. She had known that it was going to go like this, she'd even predicted the exact words her brother would use. Nevertheless she had held out hope, however faintly. Since he'd been locked in a solitary cell he didn't realize how many of his fellow travelers had since surrendered. Extremely long letters of repentance had been published in the newspapers; prominent names had denied more than just their ideas. Parì would have told him this if she thought it might influence him, but she knew that he wouldn't believe it. Or perhaps it would simply make no difference to him.

Simin, meanwhile, didn't want to listen to reason: "You tell him, Parì, tell him to ask for forgiveness, tell him there's no point to all this. Your friends Behruz and Amir were in prison for a number of months and now they're out. If you sign the letter of repentance they'll set you free. They've promised that."

She stared at her son, hoping that she might see in his eyes some glimmer of capitulation. Parì took the receiver. She didn't know what to say: with the little time remaining to them it seemed pointless to keep arguing, but her mother was waiting for her to help.

Javad turned to her. "And what about you—how are you?" He smiled at her sweetly.

Parì began to rattle off the trivialitics that had happened that day, grateful for some semblance of normalcy. She talked about renovations to the apartment, noisy neighbors, her job, and an unbearable client. She was still talking when the curtain began to fall. Fifteen minutes was not enough time. Simin, Parì, and Javad lowered themselves automatically, bending farther to not miss the last sliver.

Simin and Parì glanced one more time at the bleak gray curtain, then backed away, head down. As soon as they were out of Evin, they both felt the impulse to ruffle their clothes and veils, trying to shake off the prison smell. While they walked on the ramp of repentance, Simin said, "He didn't even ask about Abbas and Alì. I'll never understand these sons of mine."

48

American Iranians

SOME YEARS LATER I was invited to Seattle for a conference on women's rights. The speakers included Parvaneh Forouhar, a prominent political activist in the National Front, and Maurice Danby Copithorne, Reynaldo Galindo Pohl's successor at the United Nations in Iran. The main reason I accepted the invitation was to alert Copithorne to the great risks he was taking—that he was probably being spied upon—and to inform him of recent human rights abuses.

Ten days before my departure I called a former high school teacher who had moved to Los Angeles after the Islamic Revolution. I had been close with her because she'd helped me to overcome my problem with stuttering. She had forced me to speak slowly, pronouncing each word so that I stammered less; my oral examinations lasted twice as long as those of my peers, but the knowledge that I was allowed to take extra time gave me the confidence I needed. Back then I couldn't have imagined how useful it would be for me to learn how to talk in public. When my teacher realized my name was among the list of speakers for Seattle, she invited me to her home and proposed that we reunite with other Iranian immigrants. There's a reason Los Angeles is nicknamed "Tehrangeles"—a high concentration of my compatriots, after fleeing the Revolution, moved there. Following the etiquette of Iranian culture, I deflected the invitation with a *ta'arof*, meaning

I refused the invitation, and accepted only after being asked several more times.

When she heard that I was going to Los Angeles, Simin asked me to meet Abbas and then update her about him. Her son wrote her regularly and never forgot to send her a bottle of her favorite perfume for her birthday, but Simin worried about him nevertheless.

"A mother knows when something isn't right," she said, in response to anyone who tried to make her see logically. "How am I supposed to believe what I read in some letter or what he tells me on the telephone?"

I hadn't seen the general for years and was happy for the chance to see him. Simin said she would give me "some provisions" to take to him. The day of my departure she handed me a twelve kilogram bag filled with Abbas's favorite foods: peas, fava beans, greens, fruit, dried lemons, pistachio nuts, and our traditional candy, *gaaz*.

So my brief trip to Seattle became a long pilgrimage to visit the American Iranians—old friends, acquaintances, and even strangers, united only by the fact that we were born in the same country. I was always moved by the intensity of the ties that form spontaneously in eastern cultures, where a distant kinship or an even more fragile pretext is enough to establish a sense of common purpose.

My teacher provided me with immediate evidence of this. She was the first to rise to her feet and applaud my speech at the conference: her eyes sparkled with pride at the fluidness of my discourse and the assuredness of my tone.

"Shirin, I have to say I did a good job with you. You've become an excellent orator."

"Really, Professor?" I asked, gratified. Deep down, after more than twenty years, she still considered me one of her students. And I still called her professor.

THE NEXT DAY ARYA PICKED ME UP to take me to San Diego, where Abbas was living. The last time that I saw Arya, before he left to study in America, he was an awkward, smooth-cheeked boy, so tall that he seemed always in danger of falling over himself. The years had endowed him with an athletic, slender physique, and the easy smile of a man confident of his charms. He had his father's black hair and dark eyes, but his face preserved the gentleness that Abbas had lost by growing up too fast. He wore clothes of the finest quality and seemed completely American; the one concession to his origins was the black, well-trimmed beard, and his melodic English accent, which he couldn't quite shake.

It's about two hours by car from Los Angeles to San Diego, but the trip passed quickly as we chatted about old memories. Arya was a busy man: while still in college he had found himself an apprenticeship at an architectural firm so that he could learn the trade and get experience early on. Now, just a year after his graduation, he was already working on his own project: he and an associate had started their own firm, which was dedicated to renovating and selling old houses. As he explained to me with pride, it was an extremely challenging, and profitable, business. The American word "business" recurred frequently in his speech, though he seemed unaware of the fact that he was introducing an American term into Farsi.

His associate had recently financed a new investment: They had bought land in the Los Angeles suburbs where they were constructing a series of small houses that they expected to sell at a high profit. Arya worked a lot but he liked it, and above all he enjoyed not having to report to anyone but himself. He seemed successful and satisfied with his accomplishments.

"So when do you think you'll get married?" I asked him, mentally checking off the first of the thousand questions that Simin had wanted me to ask.

"And why should I? Here it's not like Iran, where everyone gets married because their parents expect them to. In America everyone is free to do what they want, like ignoring traditions if they want." He stared at the road. All of a sudden his voice had become veiled and I wondered if he was becoming upset for some reason.

I tried again, saying that marriage in Iran is also based on personal choice: even me, a woman much older than him, married a man who I loved without any restrictions. His face, however, indicated that he still thought differently. Abbas had likely tormented him enough with this line of conversation; it was useless to push him any further.

I moved to the neutral ground of literature and was greatly surprised to discover that even though Arya had lived for years in America, he was familiar with contemporary Iranian writers. He confided in me that he wrote once in a while: Sweet, musical poems, a few of which he recited to me. They were permeated by nostalgia for his homeland.

"You're really quite good. Have you ever thought of publishing?"

"I sent some poems to a literary journal in California and they published them. The English ones, obviously; the poems in Farsi I keep for myself and for the few who can understand them."

I regarded him with sincere admiration: Despite being so

young, he had built a promising career for himself in a new country and even showed a surprising talent for poetry in two different languages. All the sacrifices that Abbas and Touran had made
to keep their children abroad had been well worth it, I thought.

"And Borna? How is he? What's he up to these days?" I asked.
I had just realized that Arya still hadn't mentioned his brother.

Arya started scratching at his beard with obvious embarrassment. "Borna's up to no good. At first he wanted to be a film
director, then he discovered that it took a lot of hard work so
he gave it up. He never finished at the university: he studied just
enough to get by, but only lasted until his sophomore year. Leave
it to Borna—he kept changing jobs every two or three months,
and was so unreliable that he was fired wherever he went. He
only stopped squandering his money when our parents came to
America. They lost everything in the Revolution—they couldn't
even pay my mother's medical bills."

I didn't know how to respond. His tone was hard and full of
scorn, like Abbas's so many years before when he spoke of Javad,
referring to him as "that one."

"Here's an example of the kind of thing he did," continued
Arya. "When he was still pretending to be a student, he gambled
away his entire college savings in Las Vegas. He called our father
in tears, saying he'd had an accident and would be in huge trouble
if he didn't pay up. Dad scraped together what he could to pay for
my brother's recklessness. If I knew what was happening, I never
would have let him do it." Arya kept scratching his beard, staring
forward, his hands squeezing the steering wheel.

"Are you sure that he didn't learn his lesson? Sometimes all it
takes is a shock like that to set a person on the right path," I said,
trying to calm him down.

"He works as an emcee at a local nightclub. He introduces each night's acts and tells lame jokes between sets. He calls himself a director. He barely makes any money, but he's happy because he eats and drinks for free and all his friends come see him every night in the club. The job isn't much, but at least he's been able to hold onto it for a year. When he can't pay his rent, he knocks on my father's door. No, Shirin *joon*, I don't think he's learned anything."

He didn't stop playing with his beard for the rest of the trip.

"SHIRIN *JOON*, WHAT A PLEASURE to see you." Abbas opened the door at the sound of the doorbell, as if he had been waiting for me right there. It was clear that he had prepared for our meeting. His hair was combed in an orderly manner, though a few wisps tended to fall down; Abbas put them back in place mechanically, with a clean sweep of his hand. He wore a pair of black, impeccably pressed pants, and a cream-colored shirt similar to those that he had as a child. His build was the same—tall and lean—and he had the same luminous smile.

"Abbas *khan*, the pleasure is all mine! How long has it been?"

"Too long."

"You look great."

"Shirin, you're as sweet as always," he replied, remembering the old pun he'd used as a child. In Farsi, "Shirin" means "sweet."

He moved aside from the door and welcomed me into the foyer. The speckled gray floor, which continued into the hallway, was covered by a large, colorful rug. Two Bordeaux chairs, arranged next to a table, occupied the center of the room. In the left corner, near the front, was an old television set covered by a doily. Completing the décor was a waxed sideboard, on which stood a bunch of fragrant carnations. Everything was fresh and clean.

Arya said his good-byes and left to take care of some business. He promised that he'd be back soon with the city's best *chelow kebab*.

"*Chelow kebab*? You've got it all, Abbas *khan*," I said, stunned. Every object in the apartment could have been bought at a bazaar in Tehran.

Abbas looked at me with a sad smile, "You can find Iranian things, but objects aren't everything. In fact they barely mean anything: they lack the warmth and community you find in Iran."

While he was making tea, I sat on a chair that someone, probably Touran, had cushioned with a headrest and embroidered armrests. I sunk deep into the chair and finally felt, after days of running around frenetically, that I was able to relax. The white wall in front of me was dominated by photographs of Hossein and Simin's wedding; directly beside it were photos from the wedding of Abbas and Touran.

"I left space for Borna and Arya," said the general, following my glance. He brought in a large pewter tray and rested it gently on the table. "But Borna, that good-for-nothing, will never meet anyone. I'm only grateful that my poor Touran isn't here to see her firstborn reduced to such nonsense."

Touran had died a year after the operation, worn away by the pain of cancer and tormented by concern for her family, who were now lost without her. Abbas kept a photograph of her as a young girl on the bedside table, on the side of the bed where she had slept. Every morning and every night he said a private prayer for her.

"Arya, he's got things figured out," continued the general. "A boy like that doesn't have to look hard for a girlfriend." His eyes brimmed with pride. He started to tell me again about his son's surprising accomplishments, the work he'd done already and his promising prospects. As he spoke, Arya's architectural firm became envisioned as a giant construction company that built entire neighborhoods of skyscrapers.

When Arya had walked with me down the narrow hallway of the apartment, which was filled with indecipherable smells from the neighbors' kitchens, he told me that he had offered his father a deal on a more comfortable home. He wanted him to move into a small house that he was building, but Abbas opposed the idea in a tone that forbade any further discussion. In this example of Abbas's boorishness I saw once again a man so blind that he would lose his brothers rather than sacrifice his sense of pride. I hoped that the same thing wouldn't happen to his sons.

While Abbas was speaking, I heard a chair squeak and a television switch on in the next room. The monotonous hum that came through the thin walls was a constant soundtrack, interspersed with the metallic noise of cutlery. From the window you could see an interminable series of apartment buildings, each one the same as the next, painted in faded pastel colors. A few small kids played on the street, yelping and crying out every so often.

Suddenly Abbas's neat apartment appeared to me in a different way. On the furniture's smooth surfaces you could see, in the light, the ring stains of glasses and bottles. The embroidered headrest strategically covered spots in which the chairs had been worn away, and the table probably covered a ragged section of the rug. In the corner of the room there were small cracks in the walls, barely hidden by the curtains. Abbas's efforts to give the room a sense of order and cleanliness, a representation of his last shred of dignity, made me much sadder than the apartment's general state of neglect.

Abbas spoke to me a long time about Touran's illness, about her death and the void that it left behind; he told me about the debts he incurred trying to pay for health care, of his financial problems and his continuous sacrifices. I was stunned at the ease with which he returned to the intimacy of old times, when he was like an older brother to us children. To make a living he was now working as a baker. A former schoolmate had gone into business with him, and every morning, at four o'clock, he woke up and drove across town to knead dough and bake white bread.

"Have you ever heard of a general becoming a baker, Shirin?" he asked me. His tone was ironic, but free of bitterness. He hated his new life and his new country, but it was impossible for him to return. When he came to visit his sons, he thought that he'd still have time to go back to Iran and fight. But the shah had given up too quickly and fled, abandoning Iran to chaos. Abbas, one of the shah's most faithful generals, was left with a sense of guilt for what he now considered to have been desertion.

During that frantic period he'd tried to rush home, but the airports had shut down to impede Khomeini's return and Abbas had to watch, from a distance, as his world came to an end. He and Touran had gone to America with enough clothing for fifteen days, and now they found themselves alone, and penniless. All their possessions had been confiscated, their bank accounts frozen, their house seized. What was left for them in Iran? Besides, what was the point in returning to a country that didn't bear any resemblance to the one they'd known? Abbas realized, too, that the second he set foot in Iran he'd be executed without a trial.

"My only regret is not having taken with me a handful of dirt from my house. The shah, at least, thought of that. But of course I didn't know that I'd never see Iran again. I'd like to be buried there. I wasn't able to take Touran back. Perhaps, when it's my turn, we'll both be able to return together." Abbas was staring at a fixed point on the wall over my shoulder, the cup of tea going cold in his hand. Thin lines appeared on the corners of his mouth and around his eyes. He had stopped smoothing the ruffled wisps of his hair and let them hang over his forehead. I noticed a number of gray hairs that I hadn't seen before. He wasn't even fifty years old and already he seemed like an old man.

I asked him to tell me why, in 1979, the army had abandoned the shah. He started to speak in a flat, colorless voice.

"Don't you remember what happened? Public demonstrations every day, hordes of people in the streets, slogans filling the air. 'Allah akbar, Allah akbar!' they yelled from the windows, from the roofs, from their cars, from seemingly everywhere. They also were yelling, 'Death to the shah!'—those traitors. There were strikes for weeks and the economy was on its last legs. Here we were, a country of oil wells, without oil. Businesses were closed—they'd even closed the bazaar. People were hungry and the soldiers, the few that were left, were useless.

"There were images of Khomeini everywhere. He riled up the people and sent them to fight while he relaxed in Paris with his bodyguards. You know that the French, Americans, and British treated him as if he were already head of state?

"They ordered us to suppress the demonstrations, but what could we do? We were hundreds against their thousands. We descended upon the squares, armed in antiriot gear, and we watched the people marching. We weren't the least bit scared.

Until, that is, they started to shoot at us, and we fired back. I saw the square afterward. So many corpses, young and old, lying all over the asphalt. Some of the men on the ground had been dis-emboweled, their eyes opened in horror, while others looked as if they were peacefully sleeping. Blood pooling in disgusting, red-dish clots, was covered by flies. Much of the blood drained into the gutters and for weeks the city stunk of it.

"The others—the protestors—ran, terrified, like mice into the courtyards of the nearby buildings, they climbed through the windows and they knocked down front doors. I can't begin to imagine how many we would have flushed out if we'd done a house to house search. But nobody ordered one. The rioters who survived were splattered with the blood of their fellow citizens, and the smell of fear. They escaped, and none of them stayed behind to collect the bodies. We were the ones who mourned the young men who had been corrupted by the communists or the mullahs. We were the ones who mourned the honest families who had lost their sons.

"Then they ordered us to stop shooting. I thought that was a good sign, that a dialogue had begun, but in fact it was already too late. Unbelievable. The people were furious, and they believed in Khomeini, not the shah. Idiotic goats!" Abbas ended his long, droning monologue, shaking his head, still incredulous. He'd never figured out why Iran had rebelled.

"Why did the shah leave? If he had remained, he might have been able to defend the monarchy, or else died a hero's death. Then, perhaps, his son would have succeeded him." I said this in an effort to lift that fixed, dull expression from his eyes, rather than out of a desire to start a debate. It had never been possible to reason with Abbas.

"Shirin," he said, in a paternalistic tone, "you never understood these things. He was sick and needed care. If he remained, we would've continued to shoot, killing even more young people. He did it for them, he sacrificed himself to avoid a massacre."

"I don't understand, Abbas *khan*. If the shah knew he was very sick, he shouldn't have feared dying in defense of the throne. As for the massacre, don't you see how many people die there every day still? The dissidents, or those suspected of dissidence, are captured, tortured, killed. Do you know how many executions have been ordered since the Revolution? How many kangaroo trials? How many deaths?" I still had the speech that I'd prepared for the Seattle convention fresh in my mind and, in my heart, a sense of desolation at the knowledge of my powerlessness.

"Shirin, that wasn't the shah's fault—it was Carter who abandoned us. Shortly after Touran's operation, in December or maybe January, they called an urgent meeting for the military's chiefs of staff, at seven thirty in the morning. We met to discuss the political situation, and our options for defeating the revolution.

"When I arrived, the military's top command was already there, a large group on whose loyalty I would have sworn to the end. Only later, when I left the country, did I realize that a few members had been missing, including some people I had known for years. The traitors, generals like me, had already packed their bags and fled before the whole ship went under.

"One of the men among us that day, however, was Huyser—General Huyser—sent from the United States to make sure that the situation was kept under control. Hah! He was only there to make sure our hands were tied. He rose, in the middle of the meeting, and said, 'The military can't intervene. Too many soldiers are believers and they'd revolt. Khomeini has a major influence on them. Defections in the barracks don't matter, but if the army gets involved, a civil war will break out.'

"No one spoke. How could we allow that American to make our decision for us, especially when that decision was to surrender? But Huyser didn't seem to care. He said, 'At the Guadalupe Conference, the United States, England, France, and Germany all agreed. We have to prevent a civil war. Iran has too many advanced weapons, jets and missiles—it'd be a massacre. And the weapons would end up in the hands of the Soviet Union. If, instead, we can reach some agreement with the leaders of the revolution, then we won't lose the military.' That was his idea: reconcile with the revolutionaries."

Abbas never had an objective position on politics, and even now he couldn't view what had happened with detachment. His rancor and discouragement were as vivid now as during the time of the Revolution.

"I listened to Huyser's raving and I waited for someone to silence him. But no one did. Finally I stood up. 'General, you're asking us to betray His Majesty. How can you possibly expect us to accept your conditions?' I waited for someone else to support me, but the commander of the chiefs of staff gave me a stern look and signaled for me to sit down: 'Certainly we are loyal to the shah,' he said, 'you don't doubt that, do you, General? But it's in the interest of the nation, and the royal family that we remain neutral. And so we will.'

"'Staying neutral means giving the country over to Khomeini's mullahs,' I replied. The head of the air force asked whether the shah had agreed to these measures. The commander of the chiefs of staff responded that His Majesty was too sick—we couldn't put his health at risk with such displeasing news. Huyser agreed.

You see, Shirin? They didn't even have the courage to tell him that they were abandoning him. For the first time I was ashamed to wear my uniform.

"When I left, I thought about killing myself. I couldn't bear the dishonor of betraying His Majesty. But when I returned home and saw Touran, I couldn't go through with it. She still needed me. I couldn't leave her. So I turned my back on everything and I left. I have to confess one thing to you, Shirin: when I took that airplane to Los Angeles, part of me knew that I'd never return, that I was abandoning my country just like all those traitors had. Perhaps it's only right that I've become a baker," he concluded wearily, "because I'm not a good general."

"Abbas *khan*, you couldn't have saved the country by yourself," I said, trying to console him. "The Iranian people had been worn down by too many years of violence and abuses of power. The only hope was that the shah would step down and prepare the way for his son's succession."

Abbas leapt to his feet. "Shirin, you haven't been listening to me. I just explained to you that the shah had no choice. It was all the fault of the United States, which abandoned their most loyal and important ally in the Middle East. You don't believe me?" he said to me, giving me a challenging look.

Deep down I thought that Abbas wouldn't be able to hold the shah accountable for anything. Even if that meant blaming America entirely.

Seeing the disappointment on my face he went over to the sideboard and took out two dog-eared books; as he flipped through them I saw that many passages had been underlined.

"Look, the Americans themselves admit that they brought down the shah," Abbas said passionately, shoving the two books in my face. "It's all here. In his memoirs, the ambassador William Sullivan acknowledges that the United States advised His Majesty to leave Iran—that it was in his best interest, and the country's. The ambassador delivered the message himself. And the shah trusted him and said only, 'Very well, but where should I go?' Even Huyser tells the same story. Look here."

He opened General Huyser's book, *Mission to Tehran*, and pointing to the underlined sentences, repeated, "See, he admits it. He was assigned to Iran with the purpose of convincing the army to proclaim itself neutral, in order to prevent a coup. And think, only a few months earlier Carter had visited and reaffirmed his support for the shah! They treated Iran like Aladdin's lamp: they thought that if they'd rub the country a little, they'd awaken the genie. Now they don't know how to get rid of that monster, they can't control him and they're afraid. *Now* they're afraid. It was Carter, that traitor—it's his fault, not the shah's. You're still drunk on communist ideas."

In almost any other circumstances I would have fought back and said that the United States had always controlled and manipulated us, even during the reign of his precious shah. I would have brought up Mossadegh and our old debate. But I was too happy to see him cast off his defeated look, and his cheeks had regained their color, so I let it go. The belligerent Abbas that I had known had returned, at least for a little while.

It had been difficult to suppress a laugh when he mentioned the communists: For him, anyone who was antimonarchist was a Marxist. This was how almost all of the shah's supporters, at least the few that had survived, saw the world. They were called "*Shahollah*," the shah's party, in contrast to Hezbollah, the party of God—a term that we used to describe Khomeini's most rabid supporters. Abbas's thoughts had never evolved past the military academy, where he had ingested the throne's propaganda. Parì had been right: her brothers lived in a cage that even history could not unlock. Especially history.

Abbas continued his invective against the United States. "They talk about human rights, but look how they treated the shah. They didn't even let him in the country to receive medical treatment. Carter said that if he did, he'd be going against American interests because he would irritate the new government. They only allowed him in at the end, when it was too late."

I let him vent until Arya rang the front door. I was happy for the interruption; it was becoming too difficult to listen in silence to Abbas's blind defense of the shah. And Abbas didn't give me any chance to change the subject.

We ate San Diego's best *chelow kebab*, chatting cheerfully as we did. While Arya did the dishes, Abbas offered to show me some photographs. As I watched him open a drawer, looking for a photo album, I saw the metallic glimmer of a revolver. When he saw what I was looking at, he tried to downplay it. "Oh, it's just an old memento, Shirin. Why—what did you think?"

"I think it's insane, Abbas *khan*. You know what they say about Iranians in America—and here you're hiding a weapon in your house?"

"It's my old pistol," he said curtly. "In the military they taught me that a soldier's dignity is from his weapon. And even if I'm a baker now, I was once a general for His Majesty."

Abbas took out two photo albums and we flipped through them together: family snapshots, lunches at the big house in Abbas Abad, photos of the brothers when they were little; we saw the faces of so many childhood friends that we'd forgotten over the years. I felt a lump in my throat at the thought of how many of those cheerful faces and young bodies were now underground.

One black-and-white photo slid between the pages and fell to the ground. Abbas picked it up and glanced at it—it was a picture of him and Javad playing soccer. Abbas was an adolescent, tall and corpulent, his eyes on the ball; his younger brother was jogging behind him, his curls disheveled by the movement, a smile on his face.

Abbas put the photo back in its place without saying a word.

"Javad's in prison again," I muttered, unable to keep my thoughts to myself.

"Yeah, I knew that. I always told him not to follow that path, even since he was in school. And he wouldn't listen to me. Look at the result: he's caused years of suffering for our mother, he married an even worse fanatic than himself, and now he's in prison again. Only this time no one will be able to save him."

Despite his age and the political issues at play, Abbas still spoke of Javad in the same irritated manner as he did twenty years earlier, when he had been first surprised to find Javad reading Marxist essays.

"Parì and Simin were trying to convince him to ask for forgiveness. They did what they could."

"He'll never ask for forgiveness, not Javad. He was always stubborn and he's not going to change now. He's forsaken his family for his beliefs, so why would he sacrifice his beliefs for them now?" His voice was filled with a mixture of disdain and pride. I wish he could have seen how similar he was to Javad.

* * *

ABBAS WALKED ARYA AND ME to the car. We parted warmly and he said he hoped I'd visit him again.

"Shirin *joon*, when you come again, please remember to take a little bit of Iranian dirt with you. I'd like to put some on Touran's grave."

He gave me a package for Simin and letters for Parì and some old friends. Only then did I remember the bag of provisions that I'd left in the car. Fortunately there wasn't anything too perishable. I pulled it out of the trunk and gave it to him.

"Here you go, something special from your mother. It's all of your favorite things, General, straight from the bazaar."

At the sight of that package of fruits and vegetables somewhat crushed from their trip across the ocean and the United States—his eyes moistened and a few tears dropped silently down his cheeks. I'd never seen him cry before.

"Thanks, Shirin. You've made me very happy."

On the way out, as we turned the corner, Abbas called out to me again and began running after us.

"Shirin, one more thing. When Parì cleared out my apartment, did she take Mossadegh's pen? It was in the top drawer of my desk." He was out of breath.

"I don't know, General. But the desk was in bad shape so they left it there. I'm sorry."

"It doesn't matter, it was just a stupid memory. Nothing more than a stupid memory now."

19
Ruhollah's Song

"COMMANDER!" someone yelled.

Alì was leaning against an armored tank, smoking. He turned around slowly to see who was calling him. It was a new recruit, one of those kids from a bad neighborhood who still hadn't figured out how the military hierarchy worked. At least he was enthusiastic.

The boy stood before him, red-faced from the exertion. Only then did Alì understand.

His first thought was for Mariam and his son. He recalled how she cried from happiness on the day of their wedding, and again when Ruhollah was born. In traditional families, having a son was considered a great blessing, and she, like all respectable women, had always expected to become a mother. She became pregnant a year after their wedding and Allah had now given her a son. She started crying soon after he was born, and she didn't stop until the following evening. Alì had been proud of her when she tried to stifle her cries of pain during labor, but he was even more proud when she wasn't able to hold back her tears of joy.

Mariam didn't cry on the day she'd left their apartment in Tehran. It was 1981, and Alì had been fighting for a couple of months in the country's southern region, countering the most violent Iraqi assaults. They wanted to stay close to each other— and it was a wife's duty to follow her husband, after all. So she took Ruhollah, who had just learned how to walk, to Ahwaz. Alì, who had become his battalion's commanding officer, was able to stay with his family two nights a week, at least when he didn't have to go out on special missions.

Mariam and Ruhollah rented two rooms in the soldiers' compound in Ahwaz. The only furniture in their tiny apartment was a rug and some cushions, on which Alì, when he visited, lay on for hours, in an effort to soothe his back pain. He was satisfied with the direction his life had taken. He dedicated all of his time, and his body, to the defense of his country, which had been attacked by Saddam Hussein without warning. His wife and son were nearby and, at least early on, he was in regular contact by mail with his mother.

As soon as that first helicopter had dropped him off, he knew that he was doing the right thing. He looked around, shielding his eyes from the dust, and prayed for the safety of all the soldiers, and for their commanding officer to show them the right way. He prayed again a few months later, when he became commanding officer himself.

His love for the Revolution and for Ayatollah Khomeini had enriched a life that might otherwise, in his view, have been empty. But he didn't realize that his religious fervor had transformed him into a stubborn man who couldn't make sense of any ideas that weren't in line with the Revolution, Islam, and the orders of his superiors. It took the arrival of his wife and son to give him a new capacity for tenderness, an aching sentiment of which he was ashamed, and which overwhelmed him as soon as he removed his helmet at the entrance of their small apartment. He waited for Ruhollah to run over to him with his unsteady gait. Then he lifted his son in the air to hear his shrieks of joy.

"Up, *Baba*, up," said Ruhollah, with an imperious tone. He put the boy on his shoulders, and Ruhollah spread open his arms and pretend to soar. He took that image with him to the front, when the Iraqi airforce bombarded the cities and their bases, when all he wanted to do was curl up into a ball and hope for the best. The sound of his son's warbling voice in his head drowned out the roaring motors and the thunderous explosions of the bombs. Without even realizing it, that litany of baby-talk had gradually replaced his regular invocations to the heavens.

He wrote to Simin during his breaks, while sitting in the shade of some military vehicle. He wrote about little Ruhollah's progress, his wife's volunteer work, though not much about the war—he knew most things wouldn't make it through the censors. But after Javad was arrested again, he wrote less frequently, worried that he might be "contaminated" by his traitor brother. He still wrote once in a while, only because he knew that his mother would have troubles if she stopped receiving his letters; he wrote them methodically, out of a sense of duty, and it became one of his many obligations in the military. The letters depicted soldiers eating and sleeping, under a sky that was nearly always blue and clear—almost cheerful—unchanged since the day he arrived. It was easy to forget that he was risking his life every moment, that the men under that blue sky were fighting with real weapons and bled real blood, that they were fighting to advance the front—or simply just to avoid death.

Perpendicular to a line of parked armored tanks, there often also formed a line of soldiers on their breaks; they lay on the ground head to foot, their feet bare and their heads covered to shield them from the sun, and tried to get some sleep. They prized these moments of rest; sleep was even more valuable than food.

Mariam had started volunteering at a center that provided assistance and provisions to soldiers, and after a few weeks she became the chief of her department. She was inexhaustible, she worked with the same dedication that she devoted to her family and that she had seen in her husband. She cooked for hours and mended uniforms; there was always something to do and she took under her direction two other girls, who helped wash the vegetables and cook the rice, and collected clothing from the people in the nearby cities. Alì was proud of her. When she came home he hugged her and thanked Allah for having given him such a devoted, energetic wife.

The Iraqi military, which had a superior air force, body armor, and heavy and light artillery, created problems for Iran's defense; in the first months of the war Iran was forced to surrender the cities of Abadan and Khorramshar. Ahwaz was the next target. The bombings left almost nothing standing. Wherever you looked, you could see piles of brick and rubble, braids of electrical wire, empty casings, warped metal, walls split open. Everything was coated in desert dust.

Mariam and Ruhollah had escaped those huge attacks of the first two years unharmed, and now, with the shifting battle lines and the Iraqi's partial withdrawal, they almost felt safe. When Alì left the apartment and returned to the front, he gave his young son a deep look, and said, "Listen here: you take care of your mother while I'm away." Ruhollah nodded as if he understood his responsibility.

But Ahwaz remained Khuzistan's principal military base and Iraq started a new round of bombing in 1985.

*   *   *

"COMMANDER," SAID THE SOLDIER.

Alì imagined his wife under a pile of rubble, covered with blood.

"What is it?" he asked, trying not to show any sign of weakness.

"Commander, the soldiers' compound in Ahwaz was destroyed by the Iraqi air force."

A shiver went down his spine at the thought of Ruhollah's defenseless body.

"Yes," replied Alì. "Thanks for informing me."

The boy left, uncertain whether the commanding officer had understood what he'd said. But then, when he glanced back, he saw the commanding officer collapse at the foot of the armored tank, and realized that the message had come across.

It had been impossible to find their bodies. Two houses had been demolished; they collapsed into a nearby building, and then poured onto the street. The two rooms with rugs and cushions no longer existed. All that remained was a pile of rubble. Houses, once they're demolished, all look the same. This is also true of people.

Alì ordered his division to dig out the site, but after a day and a night of searching the solders were showing signs of giving up. They'd been digging for him, in the hope of finding at least the remains of his family, but their respect gave way to pity when, after two days, he had yelled at them to keep going, that his wife and son had to be there—that they were still alive. It was dark before Alì finally gave up. A glance from one of his soldiers had convinced him. He looked at Alì the way one would look at a man with a terminal illness, or an elderly man who had lost his wits. Then he got up and stretched his legs, which after crouching for so many hours hurt as badly as if they'd been broken. He took off his helmet and said, "Let's go back to camp."

He hadn't even found a piece of fabric, a trinket, or a splinter of furniture that he could put in his pocket and carry with him onto the battlefield.

Alì didn't say anything to his mother for more than a month. He felt dead and invincible at the same time. He put himself in the most dangerous expeditions, he was the first to open fire, he volunteered for every mission.

He threw himself into the arms of death, but death didn't want him. For every action he received praise and a medal. At the end of each skirmish he looked to see whether he'd been hit, but each time he discovered that, despite his best efforts, everything was in its right place, and mere scratches couldn't begin to compensate for his pain. The next day he would begin all over again, and the day after that. Then he determined to do even more and drew on reserves he never knew he had; he never tired, never took breaks next to the armored tanks, never looked up into the blue sky. All he cared about were weapons, helmets, camouflage fatigues, bullets, missiles; he never spoke to anyone. And never even took time for prayer—he worried that an incantation might blot out the sound in his head of Ruhollah's joyous voice.

20

The Final Betrayal

TRADITIONAL IRANIAN FUNERALS are held in mosques: a mullah recites a few verses from the Koran and speaks at length about the deceased, then he prays for the soul to pass in peace over the *pol-e sarat,* the bridge that connects the earthly world to the hereafter. The relatives pray with him and those who were closest to the deceased are invited to the family's house to share memories and eat halva.

After the Islamic Revolution, some Iranians' aversion to the new regime resulted in their total abnegation of religion: in wills they requested that no formal religious ceremony be held. In these cases, the mourners went straight to the family home to weep together.

Parì had organized such a gathering. Her apartment was too small so she decided to rent a large, unfurnished room, and ordered a hundred folding chairs. There were not enough available in black plastic so she had to take twenty in a harsh ruby red color that clashed visibly with the mood of the room.

My mother and I entered into the part of the room reserved for women. Heavy drapes covered windows that extended to the ceiling, giving the room a dense, milky lighting. Here and there were huge bunches of flowers tied with black ribbons. Standing on the large table in the center of the room was a framed photograph of Abbas. He had been promoted back to general. The photo was taken at a three-quarter angle, with Abbas in uniform, staring straight ahead. He wasn't smiling.

The female section was almost full: aunts, cousins, and old family friends had arrived early. The men, of whom there were far fewer, were still standing and looking around for notable guests. The ranks of the military had been decimated by the new regime's "purification" efforts and by the war. Only a few friends and fellow soldiers remained.

Nor was his family present. Javad was in prison, Alì was at the front, Borna and Arya were in America; Simin was in intensive care after suffering a heart attack at the news of Abbas's death. Parì, as always, was the only one to represent the broken family.

She tried to persuade Alì to take a brief leave of absence.

"I can't abandon my soldiers right now," he had said hurriedly into the telephone. "We're trying to stop Saddam Hussein's army." They had entered a new phase of the war; after Iraq's initial advances, Khomeini was recapturing his lost territories, and he had indignantly refused the United Nations' peace plan, hoping instead to spread further his Islamic Revolution.

"Alì, please," said Parì, but her brother interrupted her, unable to waste any more time. "I will read the entire Koran in an effort to save his soul," he conceded, before hanging up. The *click* of the severed phone line echoed in Parì's ear like a gunshot.

It was a simple ceremony. His friends gave speeches in Abbas's memory and returned to their seats in silence. Finally Parì stood up, beautiful and composed in her simple black dress. She recalled the kind brother of her childhood and the generous one of her youth, then she introduced a poet who recited a passage from the *Shahnameh* in honor of Abbas's patriotism and his love for the monarchy. Some people in the audience glanced around nervously.

At the end, we all lined up to give our condolences. My mother enveloped Parì in a heavy embrace: "I never thought I'd be around to witness the death of one of your brothers," she whispered. Then she asked about Simin.

"She's doing better. The doctor says she'll recover. Tomorrow she should be able to leave the intensive care unit. . . . I never thought this would happen either." Her voice was soft, and she spoke without hesitation, as if from a great distance. Everything about her seemed strangely detached: the perfect hair, the well-ironed dress, the light makeup, her steadfast composure.

When it was my turn I hugged Parì lightly.

"When you want to talk, you know where to find me," I said.

"Not now, Shirin *joon*, not now. Tonight I'll come for tea."

When she showed up we ate a pizza together and then put the children to bed. Once we were alone, Parì told me what had happened.

On Thanksgiving, Abbas went to visit Arya in Los Angeles. His bus got in at seven at night, in time for dinner; it was just the two of them. Borna had a show to emcee and they had no other family in America. They didn't say a blessing and they didn't eat turkey; they'd never celebrated Thanksgiving, it was just an occasion to be together. For the first time in months, Abbas didn't have to wake up before dawn to bake, and for him that was more important than any festivities.

On Sunday, the fourth and final day of his visit, Arya left for a business meeting. "I'm going to rest a little bit," said Abbas that morning, after having a doughnut with tea. "I have to go back to work tomorrow." But he couldn't fall back to sleep, and soon he got tired of watching television.

His only distraction was the courier, who asked him to sign a receipt and gave him a bank envelope addressed to his son. Abbas went to put it in the living room, on a bookshelf, where Arya kept his bills and other mail. Before turning around he saw an album—one of those old photo albums just like the one he had for his wedding, with a hard green cover and floral embroidering. He picked it up and went to sit on the couch, resting the album on his knees. There was Arya in his mother's arms, Arya yawning, Arya with a pacifier in his hand and a thumb in his mouth. Then there were photographs in which he was a bit older, reading a book while Borna played in the background. His whole childhood flashed by in a few pages, some of them taken after Touran's death. The two boys grew up, and there they were on their first day of college, standing in front of the building, just as their mother had always wanted.

As he turned the pages Abbas felt his hands and temples fill with a sudden heat. He was nostalgic for his family: he had served as father to his brothers, from whom he'd been torn by an even higher loyalty; he had married for love, but respected tradition; he loved his sons, who represented the sole meaning of his life, especially the younger one; he lived alone and awoke every morning in darkness. A grandson was the thing he desired the most—a son for Arya, to prolong the family's strongest branch. He sighed, closing the album, but keeping his place with his finger, so that he could continue going through it once this burst of heat had passed. Perhaps a girl was hiding somewhere in the following pages. A future wife to whom Arya had not yet introduced him . . .

Abbas turned the page anxiously. Two photos had come unstuck, and they slid onto his legs.

In the first, Arya and another man were hugging; in the second, they were kissing. The warmth he had been feeling turned suddenly to ice. He looked ahead of him and saw the same armchair as in the photo of the kiss. He sat motionless for a few minutes, unable to reopen the album—which he had thrown onto the ground, as if a snake had darted out of it. His fingers turned purple, and stiff. A trickle of sweat froze on his forehead, making him shiver at the draft that passed through the window. His eyes opened wide and he couldn't hold back the nausea from rising in his stomach. His son . . .

"Why don't you get married?" said Abbas, as soon as Arya came back home. He was standing, sweating again, and he stuttered as if he were half-asleep.

"Always the same questions," said Arya, taking off his jacket. "I don't want the traditional family that you want." Then he removed his shoes and started walking toward the kitchen. He was dying of thirst. Abbas went after him and said, in the same shaky voice as before, "You mean traditional like in Iran—between a man and woman?"

Arya, suddenly still and alert, turned toward his father. But there was no time for him to react. His father pounced on him, throwing something at his face and yelling: "You'd prefer a different kind of family? Why? Why?"

After they hit his face, the two photos fell to the ground. Arya caught a glimpse of them and glared at his father. He didn't show any sign of shame. Only sadness without end.

*   *   *

A FEW DAYS LATER ABBAS was watching television in his armchair, trying to sooth the pains that for months had been plaguing his bones. Waking up at such an early hour every morning, all year long, had taken a toll. He wasn't old, but he felt like he was. And just like an old man he sat in front of the TV, dozing off from time to time and then sitting up straight and forcing himself to follow the images that streamed in front of him.

Usually he watched the news and, once in a while, old movies.

From the darkness outside the window he could tell that it was night. He had no idea what time it was: it didn't really matter to him, to tell the truth, but he was beginning to get hungry.

It was a struggle to get up. As usual.

He went into the kitchen, reheated some leftovers, and ate. He glanced at the clock on the wall. It was a little past six o'clock. Soon he'd have to be at work again.

After putting the plate into the dishwasher he returned to the living room and started searching for the old photographs he'd taken with him from Tehran. He looked again at his two children, and then Touran and his brothers, who themselves were children in the photos. He had been betrayed by all of them and those who hadn't betrayed him were dead by the hands of traitors.

He rested the photo album on the front table and began to rummage through the drawers of his desk.

He thought again of Arya, Javad, Alì, Parì, his shah, Borna, his mother, his father, Touran—everyone.

Then he thought of the picture of Arya embracing another man.

He put the pistol to his temple and fired.

*   *   *

PARÌ WAS THE FIRST TO LEARN about her brother's suicide, just as she had been the first to learn that Arya was a homosexual. Arya had told her himself, during a vacation to London. Parì had advised him to see a psychologist.

"So?" she asked him, a few months later, on the telephone.

"It's better." Arya had decided not to keep his sexuality a secret, not to be ashamed of what he wanted, and he'd even found a boyfriend. It was a colleague of his, a very handsome man whom Parì had seen in a photograph. She made him promise not to say anything to Abbas. She was sure that he'd die of a heart attack if he learned that his favorite son was not only going to deny him a grandchild, but was in fact a homosexual—a forbidden word in Iran.

"Take care of yourself," Parì always told him at the end of their conversations, and she said it then, too, prepared to keep her nephew's secret and to be someone to whom he could turn for support.

Parì told me this in a subdued voice, allowing the tears to blur her makeup. The stress of the funeral arrangements was dissipating, leaving her only with pain.

"It's strange," she said slowly, "now that Abbas is dead I feel like a lost little girl. Part of me continues to think of him as a generous brother who provided for all of us. But it's been years since we could count on him. He held so tightly to the bars of his cage that he closed us out completely. Ultimately it caved in on him."

"What do you mean?" I asked.

"He was so convinced of his stubborn ideas that he couldn't accept reality. Not even Arya's reality. He's a good boy—so what if he's a homosexual?"

"Abbas wasn't ready for that. He lived in an old world, unchanged by the passage of time."

"But that's absurd. He sent his sons to study in America, how could he expect them not to change? Arya was born this way, and growing up in the West gave him the courage to respect himself." A passion was slowly emerging in her, awakening her numbed consciousness from the shock of the past days. The Parì that I knew was coming back.

"Arya can't be different from the way he is, but the same was true of Abbas. For years he had followed the military's rigid code of discipline. He was up at six, lights out at nine. His ideas were as regimented as his days. You think he was going to change when he turned fifty?" she said, in a tender voice.

Parì lightly shook her head, then rested her forehead on the edge of the table. I sat next to her and put my arm around her shoulder. She sobbed almost inaudibly, a dry, halting noise rising from her throat.

"Go ahead," I said softly, knowing that it would make her feel better. "Cry. Cry for Abbas." But without raising her eyes she gave me a firm, almost violent shake of her head.

"Abbas buried his wife and the shah, he lost his home and his country, and he discovered that his favorite son was not the man he thought he was. It's unfortunate, that's true, that he wasn't able to cope with all of this. But I'm not crying for him now. I'm crying for Arya, who adored him and whose conscience will always bear the weight of his father's death."

24

Something Warm

PARÌ WALKED THE "ramp of repentance" for the second time at the beginning of 1988. She was carrying with her a parcel of newspaper clippings, and she had spent hours preparing for the conversation she would have with her brother, who was still in solitary isolation. She knew that it would be the most important conversation of their lives.

After great effort, she had managed to obtain a one-on-one meeting. Alì's name opened many doors and she had no problems using it, even though he hadn't any idea she was doing so. She had gone, wrapped in Simin's loose-fitting chador, to plead with the president of the tribunal. Like her mother when they visited Evin before, she could be humble when it was expedient.

"*Haj agha,*" she had implored respectfully, "let me see my brother again. He's lived in isolation for years, he has no way of knowing how much things have changed. Tell him how many communists have been repentant, and how merciful you are. Perhaps he will be convinced that his ideas were wicked and dangerous." Her argument seemed to be failing, and she wondered whether she could ever be convincing. For a second, the thought of what Javad might say if he heard her talking this way gave her pause—but she dismissed it. Life was more important than ideas.

"I hope for your sake that he does," said the president crisply. He was one of the many mullahs who had ascended to a position of great power thanks to old friendships. "He has committed an extremely serious crime."

"Serious? Serious in what way?" asked Parì, momentarily losing her composure.

"You're not here to ask questions. Just do what I say." After this he sent her on her way with a curt "*Khoda havez*," and made a gesture that indicated she should leave without any further conversation. Before Parì had left the room, he had already turned to another prisoner's file.

SIMIN, STILL RECOVERING from her heart attack, had not been able to accompany Parì. She didn't want to go alone, however, so I went with her. By this point I was already retired. I couldn't bear working for the Ministry of Justice after my demotion and I'd asked for an early pension. The regime permitted me to become a housewife, so I had some free time. I didn't have the same level of clearance that Parì had obtained, so I stayed outside, observing the "ramp of repentance" from across the street.

A guard ordered Parì to enter a square room, its windows coated by a layer of filth that had built up over the years, through which the sunlight barely passed; on the windowsill there was a vase of gray-orange plastic flowers. Javad entered, escorted by a soldier. He was even thinner than before and he wore dirty convict overalls; his feet, in a shapeless pair of slippers, dragged across the ground. It was painful to look at him, but at least this time there was no wall between them, no gray curtain.

They sat on either side of a tiny table. The guard stood next to them.

"I was guaranteed a private conversation," said Parì peremptorily. She was too tired to beg. "Can you leave us alone?"

"This isn't your house," responded the guard. "We give the orders here." He stepped a few feet back and leaned against the wall. He never took his eyes off her.

"Let it go, Parì," said Javad. "Everything we say will be recorded anyway."

Parì turned back to her brother. He had aged considerably. The skin of his neck was wrinkled. His hair was a dirty gray that would soon be white. Only his beard had remained the same black as before, but now the color seemed almost artificial. The bushy hair covered his full lips and hid the jaunty curl of his smile. Javad seemed finally to have lost his childish charm. Even the vivacious black eyes, veiled by exhaustion and suffering, no longer sparkled.

Remembering their last conversation, Parì forced herself to look directly into her brother's eyes and got right to the point: "I spoke with the president of the tribunal. He said that you should ask for forgiveness, because your crime is very serious."

He raised the corner of his mouth in a weary attempt at an ironic sneer. "I only wrote a few articles for the newspaper. In no other country in the world is this a crime." He spoke clearly, in a defiant tone, making certain that his words would be cleanly recorded by the microphone.

Parì removed a few pieces of paper from her bag and set them on the table. "Look what your bosses wrote. They've repented, and pledged their support for Khomeini. Those who didn't were killed. Please Javad, open your eyes." Her voice was shaky; she realized that the word "killed" felt terribly real to her, and her breath caught.

But Javad didn't seem disturbed. He passed his hand over his hollowed cheeks and responded angelically: "I have nothing to apologize for. And do you really believe anything that's written in the newspapers these days? Do you think there is freedom, or truth, in those pages? Open *your* eyes—they're all lies."

Parì stared at the ground, at Javad's feet, almost invisible in the black slippers. The fringe of his overalls was ragged, frayed. Once it had been undamaged, new—like their family. It was this thought that gave her the strength again to face her brother.

"And what if it's true?" she asked vehemently. "If really all the others chose to live rather than rot in prison? Would that be so absurd, Javad?" For the first time she saw a fleeting shadow of doubt in his eyes. "What if all it takes to get out of here is to ask for a pardon, even it's for something that you didn't do? Aren't you tired . . ." she trailed off, out of prudence, but also to make him reflect on the suffering that he had endured, to think about what he was sacrificing and why. In reality, those last words had been directed at herself. Was it possible that Javad had no compassion for her exhaustion, her desperation? In just a few years she had lost a brother, her mother was in the hospital, another brother, driven mad by his suffering, risked his life every day, and now she had to convince this brother to save his own life.

She noticed that, despite Javad's prolonged isolation, he was not exhausted, desperate, or even impatient to return to real life. He had the same absent look as when he'd left Evin the first time. Except then, in the profound darkness of his eyes, there had been anger. It was that emotion, she realized, that connected him to the world and had allowed him to return, gradually, to life. But now there was only indifference on his face. Like Abbas, Javad had found himself without purpose and without family.

"I won't do it, Parì."

She was down to her final card, one she had promised herself that she wouldn't play. She told him about Abbas, his suicide, his funeral, and Simin's heart attack. Javad listened in silence.

"I'm sorry, I'm sorry about all of this. But I won't do it. That's enough," he said at last. "Don't you torture me, too."

At this point the guard went over to Javad and made him stand up. Their time was over.

"The next time you come, bring me a sweater, something warm," said Javad. And then, turning back to face her one more time, before the door closed behind him, he smiled, but it was as if from across an infinite distance.

"What did he mean?" The guard asked Parì, when he returned.

She turned toward him, wrinkling her forehead. "What?"

The Pasdar curtly repeated the question: "When he said 'something warm.' What was that supposed to mean?"

If she hadn't been behind the walls of a prison, beside a revolutionary guard, Parì would have burst into laughter. But she composed herself and calmly explained, "He's cold and he wants something to keep him warm. Some heavy clothes."

She had to repeat the same thing to other, higher-ranked Pasdaran who, after consulting with each other, kept asking her the same question, despite the fact that her response never changed. They thought that Javad's statement was some kind of code, and they detained her for two hours in the office. Finally they let her go.

As soon as she saw me, at the bottom of the "ramp of repentance," she ran toward me. She was still shaking. The image of

Javad's final smile had stuck with her. It was like the light of a distant star that had already died.

PARÌ NEVER BROUGHT WARM CLOTHES to her brother. A couple of months later they removed Javad from solitary isolation and led him into the courtyard with five other detainees. Six similar faces, haggard and gray from lack of sunlight. Twelve arms hanging on their sides, linked at their wrists by handcuffs. Twelve thin, disfigured legs, barely able to support the weight of their shriveled bodies. Two guards ordered them to line up against a wall. Six caved, stooped backs with overalls like a second, ruined skin attached to their shoulders and sides. Two other Pasdaran glanced, for just an instant, at these pathetic, almost inhuman figures. Then they loaded their rifles and fired. Javad had turned thirty-eight one week earlier.

Twenty days later Parì opened the door and found herself in front of a revolutionary guard. It was fortunate that Simin hadn't opened the door. The man handed her a green military backpack and recited the standard lines: "There can be no funeral ceremony, not even in private. If you follow this instruction, you will be told where the remains have been buried within a year from now. *Khoda hafez.*" The man turned and walked away.

Parì sat her mother down on the sofa in the living room and told her, without crying, that Javad had been executed. Simin braced herself. The two women, seated beside each other, slowly zipped open the backpack, breathing heavily, pressing close together in anticipation. They pulled out a shirt, a pair of shoes, a pair of green pants. Simin didn't recognize any of her son's clothes, but figured they had given them to him in prison. Then, in a pocket, they found a photo of a woman. It wasn't Fariba. Parì looked at the label attached to the backpack; Javad's name had been written in messy, perfunctory handwriting. And then she understood what had happened. They were executing so many people that they couldn't even figure out what possessions belonged to which prisoners. The authorities had sent her a backpack belonging to another man.

Just one week earlier, three thousand political prisoners had been killed. It wasn't the first mass execution, and it wouldn't be the last, but this recurrence of persecution had scared even some of the cleric's supporters and functionaries. Someone found the courage to distance himself from the regime and make his voice heard. The only response from the tribunal that had issued the death sentences was to affirm that every executed prisoner's case had been examined by Khomeini himself.

When Simin realized what had happened with the backpack, she gave up, and burst into tears. As her daughter embraced her, she imagined a mother in some other part of Iran opening a backpack with Javad's things. Deep down, she thought in her despair, it didn't matter whether the clothes that she was now soaking with tears didn't belong to her son. Someone, somewhere, would be crying over Javad's clothing.

22

A New Life

"TO SHIRIN, OUR BULLDOG," said Parì, raising a chalice filled with sour cherry syrup.

"To Shirin," everyone responded in chorus.

They had done everything to stop me, they had found quibbles and conflicts, they had buried my paperwork in the drawers of their desks, but finally I had arrived. After more than ten years of patience and inactivity, I was able to return to my original passion: the law. I wouldn't be a judge, of course, but at least I'd be a lawyer. I had just been awarded permission to practice law again.

I looked around me with happiness and pride. Parì had organized a magnificent surprise feast. When I had opened the door of my new office, which was still full of shipping boxes, I found myself facing my sisters, my parents, childhood friends, and former colleagues, lined up in a row, reunited to celebrate my return to full-time work. I smiled at everyone, a glass in one hand and in the other a black leather bag containing papers that they had given me. My children, with great solemnity, had presented me with the thick packet, tied with a ribbon, as if it were the most important moment in their lives.

As I was removing the wrapping I realized that they were the reason I had returned to work. My father had taught me about justice and fairness and I had passed the same values on to my daughters. But, I thought to myself, who was I to demand equality in a home that I never left? And so I returned to work, fighting like a bulldog—which is what they once called Javad—to reclaim a small corner of the law. I had become more committed to feminism as my daughters grew up. No longer was I fighting in the abstract. Now I had a concrete goal: I wanted to set an example, to devote myself to ensuring that their Iran would be better than mine.

"A champagne toast would've been more fun," Parì whispered in my ear.

"You want to give the government an excuse to close down my office before it even opens?" I replied.

"I knew that you were going to say that so I didn't bring any, but at least let me complain about it," she grumbled, making a silly face. Then she held the chalice containing the syrup up to the light as if to analyze its contents before tasting.

"You're the same old joker," I told her.

"And you're the same old bore," she replied with a smile.

Parì's never lost the sense of irony that she'd had since childhood. That was her gift. No matter how hard fate had been on her, she still had the same love for life. And her relentless optimism was contagious.

SIMIN NEVER RECOVERED from Javad's death. "A mother can't outlive her sons," she always said, and each time it was as if her back slumped a little bit more. The radiant woman who treated every guest like her best friend had been replaced by a flicker of her old self. Stricken by a kind of agoraphobia, she never left her home: Light, sun, traffic, air, people—everything became in her head the source of infinite ailments. She preferred to hide away in her dull world and pass the hours in front of the television, crumpling in her fist the lining of the sofa. She couldn't even say what she'd seen. She forgot to cook lunch and dinner, and sometimes she confused salt and sugar, cinnamon and saffron.

"My mother has become a bad cook," grumbled Parì, a smile masking her concern. "This is truly the end of the world."

She had tried to take her mother to a specialist, but after endless refusals she realized she'd have to bring the specialist to her mother. She invited a psychologist friend to dinner, with the excuse that she had to discuss work issues; she hoped that the psychologist might be able to come up with a cure. But her mother didn't speak for almost the entire night and once they were alone, Simin confronted her: "Parì, I told you that I don't want to go to a doctor and I won't. Don't try to trick me ever again."

Seeing that her ruse had been discovered, she tried to defend herself, but Simin interrupted her: "I raised four children and I spent my life trying to prevent them from fighting against each other, but it was all useless. I'm tired of fighting, and you should stop fighting, too. Leave me in peace."

It had been a long time since Parì had last seen the old aggression in her mother's eyes. She understood now that her mother wasn't confused, but was allowing herself slowly to die, a little more every day.

She tried to talk about it with Alì, but he was no help. Her brother was barely capable of taking care of himself. After the end of the war in July 1988, he had been rewarded for his services with commendations and medals, and they'd installed him in a government office, where he had a view of the entire city. Every day when he arrived at work the first thing he did was go to the large window that looked out over the street. On the wall there hung a gigantic portrait of Khomeini, who had died before he could realize his dream of a United States of Islam. His one attempt to export the Revolution had cost Iran more years of war, and had cost Alì his family. If in 1982 the ayatollah had been content to drive out the Iraqis and had accepted the peace accord that had been offered by the United Nations, then Mariam and Ruhollah would have still been alive, right by his side. Along with them could have been the million Iranians who were killed by chemical weapons, bombs, and eight years of uninterrupted conflict.

But there was something next to the portrait of Khomeini that caught his attention—a painting of a violent war scene. A young soldier lay on a field covered with blood and corpses. A wound had torn open his chest, yet his expression was serene and triumphant, because he was a shahid, a martyr to Allah's cause—the doors of paradise would open to him. Every time Alì looked at this, he couldn't avoid thinking about the wreckage that this depiction left behind: a mother, a sister, perhaps a wife and kids in tears, lost, despairing. He wondered why he hadn't died. Why not him, since he no longer had anything left to live for? He glanced one more time at the painting and felt sick at the thought of having to go back to filling in forms that he didn't understand.

Now that he had returned home and didn't have to reassure Simin anymore that he was still alive, he almost never went to see her. He found her apartment, crowded with furniture and memories, suffocating. Even their telephone conversations irritated him, filled with the same old lies: "I'm good, and you?" Nothing was good, not for them, and not for him.

At thirty he wondered what his life's purpose was. He didn't see that it had any. Everything that he believed in had collapsed with Khomeini's death. Perhaps it had never really existed in the first place. He worked at an exhausting job that he didn't like, pretending not to see the opportunism, the pettiness, and the corruption all around him. This was not what he had fought for, this was not why he had sacrificed Mariam and Ruhollah. He felt like it was all over for him, and he didn't care.

When Parì called or visited, he listened to her closely, but kept his distance. She was surprised to see him behave like a stranger. She tried to break his barrier of indifference, recalling memories of their past, or making jokes to try to get him to smile. But whatever expression she elicited vanished almost instantly.

"HAVE YOU EVER THOUGHT of leaving Iran, Shirin?" asked Parì. She was helping me clean up my office.

I looked up to try to discern her expression, but she turned her back to me as she lifted the glasses off the desk.

"No, certainly not. It's my country, and I love it despite everything."

"But you only have one life. Don't you think you deserve to live in a place where happiness is possible? It doesn't seem like you can be happy in Iran."

"I couldn't be happy if I knew that I'd abandoned my homeland in the middle of such chaos and challenges. If we have problems, our duty is to fix them, not flee. Otherwise what good are we? Have you ever read the fable of the 'black fish'?"

"Look, that's why it's a fable. Maybe you're right. But at a certain point you have to give up," she said softly. She straightened her back and gave me a tentative, sidelong glance. It seemed like she was looking for my approval.

"You remember Zahra?" I asked her. Zahra was one of her former classmates. Her sister worked as a secretary in the tribunal and in recent months I'd seen a lot of her.

"Sure I do. What about her?"

"Her brother was arrested for belonging to the Tudeh, too. The Pasdaran suspected that some other members of their family were involved and they wouldn't leave them alone. There was no evidence, but you know how little that matters."

"And Zahra's husband," said Parì, "do you remember him, that handsome man with the broad shoulders? He served as a pilot in the military. Did they suspect him, too?"

"I don't know. Anyway, it doesn't matter. The point is that Zahra felt that she was being watched constantly. She couldn't take it anymore. Finally she decided to leave the country. She moved to France."

"And the husband?"

"He didn't want to follow her, so he became a sales clerk or a truck driver. They divorced, after ten years of marriage."

"So you're telling me he's single," said Parì, giving me a wink.

I looked at her impatiently. "You understand what I'm trying to say. The Revolution has already torn apart so many families and has reduced the country to a state of exhaustion. Do you think Zahra can have any kind of happiness so far from her home and her people, without her husband and her family? Fleeing abroad is not a solution, you know that yourself. One must stay and fight." I was proud that the words to defend my ideas had come to me so spontaneously.

Parì didn't say anything, just chewed her lip.

"OK, I know what that look means. What's on your mind? Maybe I can be of some help."

"It's just that things at the university aren't going very well. After Javad's execution, they started to ostracize me. First there were small annoyances, like moving my classes into uncomfortable rooms or forgetting to tell me about departmental meetings. To tell the truth, I was happy to have a good excuse to miss those. But then they canceled my promotion and reduced my research funding, and then I had to release some of my assistants. Two days ago the head of the department told me that he had given one of my courses to another colleague and eliminated the other one because he was worried that my brother's communist ideas might disseminate into the classroom—he actually said that!"

"Parì *joon*, I'm sorry. Why didn't you tell me about this sooner?"

"You have enough problems already with the opening of your office. I didn't want to add any more."

"But you should have. And now you're thinking of letting them win?" I was already trying to figure out how we could fight back.

"If it were only that, I'd fight. But there's also the question of my colleagues. Most of them avoid me: they pretend not to see me in the hallway, some have stopped talking to me altogether. I'm alone, no one tells me anything, I don't have anyone to talk to. Even my former students are nervous when I run into them." She kept giving me a funny look, one that had within it an element of strange, sinister satisfaction. "Why should I fight all of this? I studied in England, I can find a job there or somewhere else. What's keeping me in Tehran? Abbas and Javad are dead. Alì is a ghost, my only nephews live in America—"

"And Simin?" I interrupted her, relieved to have found a good argument. "Your mother wouldn't be able to bear losing you."

"No, you're right," said Parì, looking down. "She wouldn't."
She began again with her mechanical gathering of the glasses.

I felt satisfied with this victory: I understood the temptation to abandon the fight, but to get better the country required
heroic sacrifices from its citizens. I started listing all the things
that we could do to help her at work. She listened and nodded,
though with little conviction. Patience, I thought. Tomorrow this
will pass and she'll be more combative.

I tried to avoid seeing the look of surrender in Parì's eyes. I
didn't want to admit that such a strong, determined person could
give in; or rather, I knew that if she gave up, I'd lose one of my
dearest friends.

23
A Long Voyage into the Abyss

"I NEED TO TALK TO YOU," whispered my husband, from the door to the living room. With a gesture of his head he indicated that I should meet him in the kitchen.

I glanced at the children, who were nestled on the couch watching television, then followed him. He'd already poured the tea, which we drank every evening after dinner.

"I've been put in charge of the new power plant. I received the letter today. You know I never wanted this job, but I thought that, given the situation in Tehran, it might be better for all of us to leave town for a while."

I was dumbfounded. We'd already discussed the job when the issue had first come up, and we both agreed he wouldn't accept it.

"What do you mean *all of us*?" I asked. "You can't possibly mean the children and I should move, too?"

He nodded.

How could I leave Tehran? I loved the chaotic, crowded, dirty city. Whenever I'd had to leave, even for short periods of time, I began to feel a powerful nostalgia; besides, now I had a job, friends, and family in Tehran and my days were always full. I had no desire to move to some small city in the north.

"And the children?" I asked. "What are we supposed to do about school?"

"Don't worry about them," he said, resting his cup on the

table. "It's no problem to change schools in the middle of the year. And you'll have more time to work on your book."

It wasn't an easy discussion. My husband looked for every reason to convince me to leave Tehran, and I kept coming up with reasons not to go with him. But through all this we were both just trying to avoid the real problem.

"It's not just the school. There are the piano lessons, the gymnastics, the English courses. If we leave now they risk falling behind."

"Shirin," he said calmly. "The children are still young. They'll have time to adjust, while if we stay in Tehran—"

"Then what?"

"Nothing . . ." he responded. "It's just that I'm afraid something terrible will happen."

There—he said it. Even if he didn't use the most unspeakable, unthinkable words. Ever since the war with Iraq had broken out, the regime had fought relentlessly against editors, journalists, and writers—against anyone who could make their voice heard through the written word. They were all enemies, except those who openly praised the new government. And the situation didn't improve after the war ended.

The easiest target was the Writers' Association, to which I belonged. The regime's newspapers denigrated its members and the *Kayhan* publication scornfully referred to us as "ancient café partisans." This term, in vogue since the shah's time, was an allusion to the refugees who discussed the miserable Iranian political situation while lounging about in cafés, delighted by the sound of their own polemics. Someone tried to sue the newspapers for libel, but no court would take the case, and obviously no newspaper would publish the Association's responses or protests.

These insults were soon followed by action. A notable translator was found dead in his home in Isfahan. Lying in full view,
next to the body, was a bottle of liquor that was thought to be
the cause of death. The family disputed the results of the autopsy
and wanted to ask a doctor they trusted to reexamine the corpse,
but they were denied permission to do this. The body of another
translator, Ghaffar Hosseini, was discovered by his neighbors in
an advanced stage of decomposition; cardiac arrest, concluded
the doctor. A writer and prominent university docent was run
over by a suspicious car that no one could remember seeing.

The most dramatic incident occurred several years later, in
1996. Some members of the Writers' Association had been invited
to Armenia to participate in a poetry conference. I was having
some family concerns, so I declined the invitation. The others
rented a bus and traveled over the mountain ranges that crossed
northern Iran. During the night, while everyone was asleep, the
driver turned onto a narrow, winding path, and took off at full
speed. The jolts woke one of the passengers, who saw the driver
open the door and dive out onto the road, while the bus headed
straight toward a ravine. The passenger had the wherewithal to
pull back on the break and the bus stopped right on the edge of
the road, its front wheels suspended over the ledge. The writers
cautiously stepped out of the bus, one by one, careful to avoid
causing any movements that might shift the precarious balance.
There was no trace of the driver. A little while later several police
cars arrived. Upon giving their statements, the victims were told
not to say anything to anyone about their "accident."

After this episode, we all knew that death was following us like
a shadow and we lived in a continuous state of alert. Every night I
scrupulously wrote down my schedule for the next day and hung

it on the refrigerator, so that if I were kidnapped my husband would be able to follow my movements more easily. I always took long, out-of-the-way routes and I got into the habit of changing taxicabs—in Tehran they function like small buses, with predetermined stops—several times before arriving at my destination.

Despite these precautions, I'd never thought that I was truly in danger. I told myself that I took these measures to ensure that nothing would happen to me. Only much later did I realize how wrong I was.

THE MASS EXECUTIONS that characterized the early years of the regime had provoked protests from the United Nations, which ultimately decided to send its delegates to investigate. In effect this was a warning that heavier sanctions would follow. The regime therefore was forced to give the international community the impression that it hadn't murdered its political dissidents—while at the same time continuing to do so. The Iranian authorities therefore formed a special operations team that was charged with secretly executing those who could no longer be publicly sentenced by the tribunals. This new process included a committee of religious elders who judged the evidence gathered by their intelligence forces on the "accused," and then decided their fate.

If the verdict was death, the special operations team—made up of agents trained in high-level military tactics, like bombing a car moving at 130 kilometers an hour—got involved. Not only had they been trained in the use of sophisticated weapons, they also had a blind obedience to every law written in the name of Islam, and the conviction that killing dissidents and dying for Islam would open the doors of paradise for them.

In this way Iran, hidden from the prying eyes of the West, managed to execute more than four hundred people. Even today, despite numerous theories, no one knows the names of the judges who signed those death warrants. But what we know for certain is that all of the executions were approved by the Ministry of Public Security.

The special operations team employed various methods. At times they administered a substance to their victims that they said was potassium, but triggered a heart attack. Sometimes they stabbed a victim and then chopped him into pieces, or ran over him with a car while he was walking in the street. Other times they kidnapped a person, and returned his corpse the next day or not at all.

The intelligence agency's tentacles stretched as far as Europe. On August 6, 1991, Shahpur Bakhtyar, the last prime minister to be nominated by the shah before the Revolution, was assassinated in his Parisian residence, where he had lived with a security detail. On August 9, 1992, the police discovered in Bonn the dismembered body of Ferydoon Farrokhzad, a famous Iranian showman and singer who was the brother of the famous poet Forough Farrokhzad. Fereydoon had been a long-time critic of the Islamic Revolution on his television programs. At the murder scene they found a very large shirt that didn't belong to the victim. Following an investigation the German police concluded that the assassin, after having committed the crime, had probably decided to change into a new shirt. On September 17, 1992, in Berlin, at a Greek restaurant named Mykonos, four prominent Kurds—who were opposed to the Islamic regime—were gunned down. The German police managed to arrest one of the attackers, an Iranian. The trial provoked major attention in newspapers and on television all over the world. The attacker was given a life sentence, but the most significant finding of the case was that the person behind the assassination was the Iranian Minister of the Interior, Alì Fallahian, who was then placed on an international most wanted list. Along with the minister, the Iranian government was held responsible for the massacre.

On May 23, 1997, Seyed Mohammad Khatami was elected president of the republic and held that position for two terms, or eight years total. Compared to the rest of the Iranian clergy, he was considered a moderate, and brought about greater freedoms of expression, allowing the press, finally, to denounce the political crimes that had occurred. But even after his inauguration, which occurred in August, the executions continued implacably.

On September 12, 1998, in Kerman, the bodies of Hamid Haji-Zadeh, a teacher and poet, and his son Karoun, who was only nine years old, were found tortured and cut into pieces in their beds. Haji-Zadeh had often criticized the Islamic Republic.

On November 18, 1998, the body of the journalist and political activist Majid Sharif was found in the desert. He had disappeared a few days earlier, after leaving his house in Tehran to go jogging.

On November 21, 1998, the bodies of Dariush Forouhar, the secretary of the Hezb-e Mellat-e Iran party, and his wife, Parvaneh Forouhar, both of whom had participated with me in the Seattle conference on women's rights, were discovered in their house in the capital. They had each been mutilated, each stabbed dozens of times.

On December 2, 1998, the poet and writer Mohammad Mokhtari was kidnapped in the street, shortly after leaving his house. A few days later his corpse was found in the desert just outside of Tehran.

Also in Tehran, on December 8, 1998, the writer and translator Mohammad Jafar Pooyandeh was shot after leaving his office. His body was found four days later in a neighborhood in the southern part of the city.

When, thanks to the newspapers' denunciations, public opinion began to reawaken, and the executions emerged, President Khatami had the ministry publish an official communiqué acknowledging that the murders had been committed by a "deviant" splinter group within the secret services, which had operated autonomously and without authorization.

The eighteen members of the special operations team were arrested and put on trial. I represented the Forouhar family in the case of the Hezb-e Mellat-e Iran party secretary who had been assassinated along with his wife. Through my investigation one of the leaders of the Iranian intelligence agency, who for a period of time had run the special operations team, told me that my name had been next on their list of political dissidents. But the executions were signed during Ramadan, and before the holiday had ended, President Khatami intervened, preventing them from going forward. If it hadn't been for the anniversary of the Islamic Revolution, my name would have appeared on the list of assassination victims.

The trial created a huge uproar and the entire leadership of the Ministry of Public Security and the secret services were forced to resign. But they were too important to be kept in prison; despite being sentenced to life, they were all pardoned and released. That's not all. A few years later one of the resigned ministers was seated as procurator general—a position that, as of this book's publication, he continues to hold.

BUT ALL OF THIS TOOK PLACE over a number of years. In 1992, when I was speaking with my husband in the kitchen, the seriousness of the situation was not yet clear and my only thought was that I didn't want to be away from my friends. I felt terribly guilty about the idea of having to sacrifice my friendships just to live in a place that wasn't so dangerous. And then there were my parents: I didn't want to be far away from them now that they were elderly and ill. We lived nearby and I visited them every day.

I began to fight back as if my husband were an adversary in court, knocking down every one of his arguments. I kept returning to the subject of the children's school; it'd be a thousand times better for them to stay in Tehran, I said. I promised him that I'd be more careful, I'd stop attending meetings of the Writers' Association, I wouldn't give interviews to foreign radio stations, and I wouldn't give the regime any further reasons to target me. I made these promises and many others as well, but my husband kept shaking his head. He was convinced that the situation had become too desperate.

"You're an egotist, Shirin! If you don't want to do it for yourself, think at least of your children. What would happen to the children if something should happen to you?" he finally asked me, exasperated by our endless discussion. He stood up, brusquely pushing aside his chair. He seemed extremely disappointed, and angry.

He had good reason to be. I'd recently received threatening letters. By this point I'd learned how to recognize the envelopes, but even though I had a good idea of what they said, I opened each one, in the hope that I'd find some reason not to be afraid, that they weren't in fact what they seemed to be: death threats.

The children appeared in the doorway to the living room, frightened by our yelling. They weren't used to hearing us argue. I ran over to hug them and felt their hearts beating quickly. I kissed them, inhaling their clean smell. I realized that my husband was right.

WE LEFT ON A GRAY WINTER MORNING without telling anyone. We didn't pack many bags because, a small, fully-furnished house awaited us. We were also worried about running into someone— we wouldn't want them to realize that we were moving. I looked out of the window, watching the city pass by, and starting crying out of rage and grief. I had just started to work again and already I had to give it up. Once more I'd have to be locked up at home with my books, unable even to see friends. My hatred for the regime was revived; this time it had stolen my city from me. My husband held my hand and gave me a smile. The children would be awake soon—it was time for me to calm down.

The new life was exactly as I'd expected: boring and frustrating. It's not only that I was becoming restless; I was also forced to lie constantly to my friends. We told the caretaker of our apartment in Tehran to leave our light on in the living room at night, and to tell visitors that we'd gone skiing in the northern mountains. Every two days I called him to find out whether anyone had phoned or stopped by. Often I had to call my friends and tell them that I was in Tehran, but too busy to go out. In this way I thought I was tricking the agents who were listening in on our conversations. Parì tried to see me several times, realized that I was making up excuses not to see her, and told me in an offended voice that I should call her as soon as I had more time. I felt a deep sense of guilt as I hung up the phone.

By the beginning of June the situation became intolerable. The children, on summer vacation, had nothing to do all day and I was even more restless than them. My husband proposed we go to Mashhad for a short visit. We were in the middle of planning the trip when I received the phone call.

"Shirin, you need to come back immediately. *Baba* is sick." My sister's voice was harried, confused. I heard individual words— "worsening," "serious," "not much time"—but I couldn't understand their larger meaning.

We were on the road less than an hour later. I wanted to scream my lungs out. I was losing my father, my teacher, the guide who, since the beginning of my law career, had helped me to solve important problems that came up, while preventing me from committing the kinds of mistakes caused by inexperience. My father had given me faith in myself, knowledge of my human rights, and the courage to defend them. He had taught me everything.

I didn't think for a second that he might already be dead, that they wanted to spare me the grief of crying alone. I didn't wonder why my mother hadn't been the one to call me, or why my sister was already back at home—I was too shocked to put all these things together. But as soon as I entered my parents' apartment I understood, from the tears of my mother and my sisters, and their black clothing, that I was too late. I felt the ground disappear beneath my feet, and it was as if a darkness had arisen from the bottom of the deepest sea to drag me down, grabbing my legs, pulling me into an abyss. I fell to the floor.

"Shirin! Shirin!" shouted my brother-in-law. But I didn't want to be conscious. I didn't want to return to myself and confront the fact that my father was no more. The convulsions and hysterical crying came next. My body shook uncontrollably. My brother-in-law gave me a sedative and my suffering ceased in a brief period of oblivion.

The next day was only slightly better. An old aunt of mine, my mother's sister, stayed by my bed. As soon as I woke up she started to lecture me. I needed to think of my mother, my daughters, they needed to be able to count on me. I nodded, hoping that would stop her rambling, but no, she kept talking. "There are two types of human beings. Those who have lost their father and those who will lose him. You now belong to the first group. So stop your suffering and try to accept things as they are."

I told her that she was right and I could tell that she was genuinely concerned about me. But my mind was working too fast. Everything I saw or thought reminded me of my father; soon the tears began to rush down my face and I couldn't stop them. For the first time in my life, I decided that fighting back was useless. With a sense of liberation, I surrendered to the emptiness.

For the next several months I locked myself in at home, refusing to see anybody. I didn't read the newspapers and had no awareness of anything going on outside. My daughters were my only consolation, but after embracing them for several minutes I soon lost patience, and sent them away. The darkness of the abyss into which I had sunk that day in my parents' living room had become a sweet, but suffocating companion to me. The more time that passed, the more comfortable its embrace.

In this state it was impossible for me to return to the city where my husband had been working. We decided to stay in Tehran. He turned in his resignation and found a new job. He hoped that the proximity of our family and friends, and above all the possibility of returning to my office, would bring me back to life. Every morning he made sure that I got out of bed and that I got ready to leave. I waited for him to go out through the front door, and then collapsed, fully-dressed, onto the sofa. I wasn't tricking him, really—he didn't think that I was all right, but he thought that, if he kept pushing me, I'd be shaken out of my condition.

On my birthday, despite that I had explicitly told everyone to leave me alone, the telephone rang nonstop. I didn't respond and finally I took the phone off the hook. I couldn't bear the constant ringing. Actually I couldn't bear any sound. That night my husband brought home a small cake and we ate dinner together, with a false, forced cheerfulness. I couldn't even pretend to enjoy myself anymore. My husband gave me a present, but I didn't want to open it. My older daughter, however, gave me a book of poetry and a beautiful notebook, saying, "So you can write poems for grandfather."

Those days the mere mention of my father was enough to send me into more mourning. My husband watched me closely, begging me with his eyes to restrain myself. I bit my lips until they bled.

"I have a better present," said my younger daughter. "I wrote you a piece of music. It's called *Shirin's Symphony.*"

She sat at the piano and began to play. I have to say that the piece was a bit off-key, but she played with such pride and concentration, moving her little hands with the grand gestures of concert pianists, that I started to smile. She was so funny and self-satisfied that I burst into joyous laughter. Her gift was precious.

The symphony didn't heal me, but that evening I thought back on how I'd behaved the last few months. I regretted neglecting my husband and my children. They were the reasons I was alive; without them I'd be lost. I held on to this thought with all my strength and began to see a psychologist who helped me to overcome my sense of loss.

I returned to being the Shirin of old—active and tireless—sooner than I had expected. I called everyone to ask how they were and if they wanted to have tea together. As I went about this round of phone calls I realized that I had been isolated longer than I'd thought. While I was mourning, Simin had suffered a fatal heart attack on the couch in front of the television. I didn't even remember that someone had told me this.

What's more, Parì had left Tehran and moved to London. But this, I was certain, she had done without telling me.

24

Give My Best to Tehran

Parì and I lost touch, pulled by our lives moving in opposite directions. As often happens in these situations, I promised myself that I'd call her, but something always distracted me and I never did. Actually, I felt anger rising in me. She hadn't been beside me when my father died, nor was I near her when Simin died. But this didn't upset me as much as her departure: she had abandoned me, our country, our fight. She had given up. I understood why she had left Iran on a rational level, but I still felt she had been selfish and irresponsible for running away from our problems. It was our duty to stay and save our country, and not just try to save ourselves. I risked my life for this cause every day. Who was she to run away?

In the late nineties I was invited to a seminar on child abuse that was being held at Oxford University; I would speak about my work defending the rights of children in my country. The prospect of going to England made me think of Parì. Should I or shouldn't I call her? I remained undecided for several days, then I thought back to our friendship, to her family, and the thing we had always said about her obstinate brothers—they had locked themselves in their cages. I realized that, like them, I had allowed myself to be trapped by my own ideology and as a result risked losing a friend.

I asked some mutual friends for her number and as soon as I arrived in England I called. I felt as anxious as a schoolgirl.

"Parì, hi, it's me," I said, my voice hoarse.

Silence.

What a fool I was, I hadn't even told her my name.

"Parì, it's Shirin," I said.

"Yes, of course. Shirin. I recognized your voice. I just wasn't expecting to hear from you."

I smiled, hearing her voice tremble as much as mine.

"How are you?" I asked.

"I'm all right. You?"

"I'm well, thanks. I'm in England."

I told her about my plans and the conference. She didn't even let me finish:

"We should absolutely see each other. I can come visit you— or, why don't you come to London? You can stay with me."

"That'd be great."

We agreed to meet after the seminar: I would be her guest for three days. She would take off several days from work. I felt energized when I hung up the phone: it was as if we'd gone back to the time when Parì and I would spend hours imagining the vacations we'd take together.

When I arrived in London Parì was waiting for me at the station. I stared out the train window, anxiously trying to spot her. What did she look like now? I exhausted myself trying to imagine how she had changed since I'd seen her—perhaps now she had a blond perm that would stand in stark contrast to her olive skin.

The doors opened, impatiently I stepped out of the train. I stood on the tips of my toes to see over the heads blocking my view. Finally I saw her in the distance. She was waving at me, I shouted with joy and she did the same. We embraced. The whole time we were on the platform we held hands tightly, as if by separating we would risk losing each other again.

I looked at her with an inquisitive eye. Parì had the same black bob as always; there were a few wrinkles around her eyes and at the corners of her smile, but it was still her. She was dressed in a simple, elegant outfit that showed off her perfect figure. She was much thinner.

"I jog every day, and make some sacrifices," she said, reading my mind. Then, gesturing toward a man who was watching us, smiling, she said, "I do it to keep him close." He was tall and well-proportioned, with bright eyes and light hair. Unlike Parì, he wasn't dressed elegantly—he wore large, sporty clothes that were a bit wrinkled—but he had a sincere, vigorous handshake, and a quality to his eyes that inspired immediate warmth. His name was Jack; his mother was Italian and his father English. He'd been dating Parì for two years.

When I learned that they lived together, I gave her a vexed look and said, in Farsi, "I thought that you lived alone—I don't want to impose. I'll stay in a hotel."

But Parì didn't seem at all disturbed by this and responded, in her usual breezy tone, "Shirin *joon*, don't be silly. My apartment has two bedrooms, and Jack is happy to have you stay with us. Right, Jack?" she said in English.

Jack nodded.

"So," said. Parì "It's all decided then." She took my hand and led me to the car.

*   *   *

Parì lived in a beautiful house in a residential suburb. From the outside the house was as gray and dull as all the other houses in the neighborhood, but inside the rooms were illuminated with vivacious colors: curtains, rugs, and upholstery in every hue of orange and red, and a profusion of large, soft cushions covered the beds and couches. Jack was an artist by profession and his paintings hung on the walls.

"He can't have that many customers if his paintings are all here," I said to Parì, teasing her.

She burst into laughter, while Jack watched us not understanding our Farsi. "If you knew anything about art history, you'd know that, with few exceptions, artists become famous only after their death. I'm waiting for Jack to die so that I can sell these and make some money off them. Unfortunately, until then, I'll have to store them here and keep my day job." She laughed again.

Jack and Parì were very much in love. You could tell from the small nuances that they reserved for each other, the intimacy of their gestures and the hidden glances they shared. Parì had stopped smoking at Jack's request, and every day he had tea with her after dinner, following the Iranian tradition. For the first time my friend looked relaxed: after years spent following her brothers and attending to her mother, she seemed finally to have found a person capable of caring for her. I was surprised to see that Jack was the joker of the two: Parì was still cheerful and irreverent, but she no longer had to rely just on her humor. Now Jack made her laugh, too.

Every night we ate in a different restaurant, with Jack and some Iranian friends of Parì's. During the day, however, the two of us went alone to cafés, stores, and museums. It was nice to stroll together aimlessly through the streets, losing all sense of direction and time, enjoying each other's company and the world around us. Parì told me all about her job and her colleagues. She talked about her recent vacations around Europe, and the people she encountered in the countries she visited, speaking always with her incomparable verve. I realized suddenly what I'd been missing.

And yet, despite our immediate connection, neither of us touched upon any serious subjects or our past together. We were tightrope walkers, trying not to fall off the wire, knowing that there was no net to catch us. And so while we might have appeared to be chatting and laughing freely, I sensed a barrier between us.

About Jack she remained buttoned up. Sure, she was happy to talk about the first time they met, their life together, his habits and artistic manias and his different way of seeing the world, and the distance between the two cultures they each came from. But she barely said anything about her feelings, or the future. I tried to win back her trust, but it was pointless. At least until one moment, while we were walking through Hyde Park, when I asked her why they hadn't married yet.

"Shirin *joon*, you'll never be a modern person. Why should we get married?"

"You'd get married if you were in Iran," I began.

"In Iran I'd be forced to get married," she replied with a shrug. "I'd also have to do a bunch of other things against my will. Nothing forbids us from getting married. But for the time being Jack and I are fine like this. We don't want all the restrictions of a traditional marriage, you see."

I was going to say that I understood her better than she gave me credit for, but she didn't give me the chance: "You think that if we got married, we'd love each other any more? That we'd be happier?"

"Marriage would make your bond stronger," I mumbled. "Jack is younger than you. Don't you worry that one day he might leave you for a younger woman?"

"It's not possible," she said with a grimace. "First of all, Jack won't leave me because he'll never find another person to pay for his groceries and rent while he scribbles about on his canvases. Second, if he ever decided to leave me, marriage certainly wouldn't hold him back. And third, if we actually did get married, he'd complain that I'd leave him for another man, one who was younger and better than him."

"And children?" I asked her, to bring her back to a serious subject. "Don't you want kids?"

She turned suddenly toward me, a gloomy expression on her face. "Shirin, why do you think that everyone has to live the same way? Why should everybody study, go to a university, get married, have children, and try to become rich? And then, when they finally become rich, they realize they're too old to enjoy their money. And you know what happens when the children grow up?" she asked.

"No."

"They leave home and they call mom and dad once a month to see how they're doing. But at that point, for the parents, it's too late, and they realize that they've lost their whole life without getting anything out of it. No, my dear, that kind of life isn't for me. I want to enjoy myself and my money while I still can, as long as I'm alive and in good health. Then I'll die."

I tried to tell her that she was wrong, that children aren't parasites but a fountain of energy and a greater motivation than anything else in life. I reminded her that it had been the thought of my children that gave me the strength to overcome my mourning for my father, to keep believing in myself and to overcome the dangers and tragedies I was facing. I became increasingly heated as I spoke. There was no subject that animated me more than my children, and the enormous joy that they had given me. Parì listened to me in silence, walking with her head lowered. When I was finally finished, she raised her head and stared at me.

"OK. There was a time when I'd wanted children. Of course there was. But you know what my life was like in Tehran. Only when I arrived here did I feel free to think of myself. By then, unfortunately, it was too late."

I felt extremely foolish and tactless. How had I let myself go on like that, when she had endured so much? How could I have been able to ignore the wounds hidden behind her carefree smile? What did I know of the sacrifices she had to make, and how hard she'd worked for the happiness that she had been able to attain? Parì started walking again, more quickly now, leaving me standing in the middle of the street. I caught up with her, trying to figure out how to apologize, but she didn't give me the opportunity. She started talking about our next stop, the Victoria and Albert Museum.

"Queen Victoria loved her husband Albert deeply—that's what they say at least. The museum has their collection of objects and art. You'll see she's wearing black in all the paintings made after her husband's death. She was as blind as you: instead of looking for a younger man, she kept mourning the rest of her life."

I burst into laughter.

That night we went to the opera. As I admired the splendor of the Royal Opera House, Parì continued with her teasing: "I realize that places like this aren't up to your standards. Only two more hours, then we can go to McDonald's!"

I laughed again. The next day, when we walked past a fast food restaurant, I sighed with relief. "How I missed you!"

"After all the chic restaurants I've taken you to," said Parì, "have you no shame?"

McDonald's actually had symbolic significance for us. In Iran, after the Islamic Revolution, all of the chain restaurants had been closed, because they were considered a cornerstone of American culture. At first the people didn't bother to protest: in every Iranian city there were plenty of places where you could find better hamburgers. But a few years later there was an effort to open a new McDonald's. The movement was publicized by the newspapers and became a common cause for the youth, who were eager for it to open. Again, the point wasn't the food, but to challenge the regime, which had imposed more heavy restrictions—such as prohibiting men and women from walking together in the street. The day that the new Tehran McDonald's opened students lined up for hours just to have a sandwich. One girl confessed to a journalist that she had been drawn in by the atmosphere of the place, because it seemed to her like she was having the same experience someone her age would be having in an American or European city. But this sense of exaltation didn't last. On the third day the Pasdaran closed the restaurant. The government declared that all symbols of American consumerism were forbidden in Iran.

I didn't really want to ask her if we could eat at McDonald's, but I confessed my nostalgia for those years at the university, when we'd walk through the streets with books under our arms, chatting with each other and our fellow students; when a man was only able to have one wife, and the mullahs were merely religious figures; when we didn't have to wear the veil, and there weren't separate seats for women and men; when the Revolution, the war, our personal troubles were still distant, and it was normal to go to the movies, to have fun, sing and be happy.

Parì understood what I meant, of course, but she kept teasing me anyway. Jack, however, who couldn't appreciate the irony of our jokes, thought that we really wanted to eat at McDonald's and gave us a look of sharp disapproval.

Parì kissed him, saying, "If you don't want it, dear, we won't go."

Then she gave me her arm and whispered in Farsi: "He's as brilliant as his paintings."

That was my last night in London. Parì watched me pack with tears in her eyes. She kept repeating: "Give my best to Tehran, will you? Give my best to Tehran!"

I turned to face her. I hesitated a moment before asking my question, but it was our last chance to break the silence of the last few years. "If you love Tehran so much, why'd you move to London?"

My friend's mouth assumed a melancholy expression. "I knew you were going to ask."

"You don't have to answer."

"Shirin *joon*," she said, searching for the right words. "You don't know what happened. In those last years we'd grown apart. But I never wanted to leave Tehran."

She sat on the bed next to me and began to speak slowly, while the tears streamed down her face, as they had on the night of Abbas's funeral service.

THE SITUATION AT THE UNIVERSITY had become unsustainable. The department director told her that, due to the political activities of her family members, it would be best for her to resign. Though feeling completely isolated, Parì refused to give in, and she stayed; sure, she had nothing more than a title, she had no funding for her research and at best she could only find work as a substitute teacher, but she was determined not to give in. One day the provost called her into his office to tell her that he had lost faith in her—that he feared she might corrupt the thoughts of the young Muslims who were studying medicine. Soon after that, word went out that Parì was promoting Marxist teachings during her classes—despite the fact that she didn't even teach classes anymore—and so the committee responsible for purging heretical professors ordered that she be fired. No other university in Iran would hire her.

At that point she decided to work exclusively out of her Tehran clinic. Parì was a good doctor and her billing rate was among the lowest in Iran, so she didn't lack for patients.

But one morning, when she arrived at work, she saw that the door had been removed from its hinges. Her framed medical degree had been torn off the wall and was lying on her desk. On top of it was a dog's severed head. The blood had congealed on the glass, it had soaked through her prescription pad, and had run down the legs of the desk in heavy drops. Parì ran out and vomited, then turned her back on the office and went home, her eyes misted over with tears. But after two hours she decided that she still wasn't ready to surrender: she marched determinedly to the nearest police station and reported the incident. The police inspected her clinic and took a statement. The officers made no effort to calm her down and told her that it would be best for her to leave town. Parì responded, as much to herself as to them, that she absolutely had not done anything wrong and she wouldn't be intimidated. She cleaned up the office, had her degree reframed and stood it on a desk right in front of the door.

A week later things got worse. One morning she walked in to find the office completely vandalized: the windows had been shattered, the blinds torn, and her medical instruments damaged. All the bottles of medicine had been emptied, the pills crushed, and the tubes of ointment had been squeezed out everywhere, on the floor and on the furniture. Her medical degree had been burned, all that remained was one corner of it, shredded, aside a pile of ash. The message was clear: Parì would suffer the same fate.

"That's when I decided that my family had already sacrificed enough heroes to their so-called fatherland. I left the office and never turned back. I realized that there was no longer anything in Tehran for me. Even *maman* was dead. Why should I stay? I wrote to a few hospitals in England and I found a good job in London. As you can see, even though I'm happy with my job and my life, every day I wonder: Why am I here? My patients and students in Iran need me more than they do here. But I had no choice."

I embraced her and held her close. We cried together now, for everything we had lost. And for ourselves.

"Stop it, Shirin, when you cry it makes me cry," said Parì, wiping her nose. "Then Jack will see me like this and run off to his paintings."

"Why don't you come to Tehran next spring," I asked her impulsively. "Do you want to?"

"I'd like to very much," she said, drying her tears, "but I'm in a delicate situation. I'm worried that if I reenter the country, I'll never be able to leave. With the brothers I have—or, rather, had—I'd probably end up on the list of people forbidden to travel abroad. It's too risky."

"Speaking of your brothers," I said stubbornly, "why don't you ask Alì? By now he must be pretty important in the Republic."

"Wait—you don't know? It really has been a long time. Alì left Iran before me. I had no idea where he was going. He packed a suitcase and left one day without telling anyone. A month later, he sent a postcard from France telling me not to worry. As if it was that easy. He's the only brother I have left."

"Alì renounced his cause?" I asked, completely stupefied.

"Oh yes. He had ended up in intelligence and had seen for himself what was happening. He said that after Khomeini's death, everything became corrupt and they lost sight of their goals. Deep down I always thought that it would be too painful for him to admit and that he'd always say the Revolution was right; but he did say it, the revolutionaries were wrong. Anyway, it doesn't matter anymore."

"At least he escaped in time."

"I hope you're right. But look at us now: all that's left of our family are him and me, and neither of us can return to Iran."

Jack found us like this, hugging and teary-eyed, talking non-stop. Parì's story had broken the barrier between us and now we were ready to resume our old relationship. Over the course of that long night we came to terms with our lost youth and with the ghosts of Alì, Javad, Abbas, and Simin. We laughed, recalling our happiest moments, and cried over the saddest ones, until daybreak.

25
Enemy of the Revolution

AFTER MY VISIT to London, Parì and I were in regular contact again. The cost of international phone calls didn't allow us to have very long, or frequent conversations, but rarely a month passed without us speaking. Our talks lasted no longer than ten minutes, but they had the pleasing and relaxing feel of our old afternoons spent over a cup of tea. We had a tacit understanding never to discuss delicate subjects, lest we upset each other in the short amount of time that we had together. We also worried that my telephone could be under surveillance.

A few years had already passed since our meeting when Parì sent me a letter—or rather Jack did. Surprised, I opened it: we'd never written each other before. There were four or five pages, written in an impersonal and harried tone, about life in London; but tucked in among the pages was a separate tightly folded letter written in small handwriting. I was amused by this ruse: if the censors wanted to read my mail, a sealed envelope wouldn't stop them.

Parì was urgently asking for my help: one of the regime's new, vast bureaucracies had ordered her to provide evidence that she still lived in Tehran and, therefore, had the right to keep her property. If she didn't appear in person at their offices, her home would be seized, just as Abbas's had, albeit for different reasons. In her brother's case, the government declared that it was authorized to confiscate all properties belonging to supporters of the shah; in Parì's case, the government would be taking possession of the property of an expatriated citizen.

During her absence, Parì had paid her doorman to help her keep up appearances so that her apartment would seem like it was still occupied. Every night he went into the apartment and turned on the lights, opened and shut the door, collected the bills, and if someone came looking for her, he'd say that she was on vacation. It seemed like an effective strategy, but evidently had stopped working.

Parì had left Iran years ago and no one had lived in her apartment since. The most amazing thing about the situation was the irrationality of the seizure process. They always gave the ultimatums to people who couldn't defend against them. That way they achieved their desired result—eviction—and at the same time allow the state to make the argument that this result could have been avoided. All the hypocrisies of the regime were on display in these property seizures.

The next day I went to see her doorman to get a better understanding of what was going on. The man invited me into his apartment and offered me something to drink. He lived in a small room on the ground floor, with a foldout couch in the corner and a modest gas stove toward the front. A table and two chairs accounted for the rest of his furniture. An old, faded curtain hid the bathroom. Everything suggested a combination of poverty and decorum—except for the lovely geranium that peeked out from the windowsill, the petals of which brushed against a photo that must have been taken at least fifty years earlier, of a woman in a wedding dress. Next to her, in another picture, was a young man laughing, wearing a soldier's uniform.

The doorman was in complete despair. He kept hitting one fist against the other, repeating, "I don't know how it happened! I really don't! The Pasdaran discovered everything themselves. The other day they showed up here and gave me this warning for Ms. Parì. I told them that she was at work and I didn't know when she'd be back, but they wouldn't listen to me."

I nodded silently, waiting for an opening. But he wasn't done. "I've known Ms. Parì since she was a little girl. I helped her poor mother move. They're such good people. I did everything that she told me to do."

He had worked as a doorman his entire life. For him this was much more than an injustice. In his eyes I could see that he had taken this as a personal failure. Whatever honor and pride he felt, had now been trampled upon by the fury and greed of the Pasdaran. I tried to reassure him, saying that Parì knew it wasn't his fault. But he refused to accept this. He even offered to reimburse her, in small installments, the money that Parì had paid him for his work. My heart ached for him.

That night I spoke with Parì and asked her to give me the names of some old friends of Alì so that I could get in touch with them. We both knew from experience that the most efficient way to resolve a problem like this was to appeal to an official in the new regime; following the established legal avenues would be useless. Parì gave me the names of five influential people who might be able to help.

The next day I began my research. The first of the five had been the victim of germ warfare during the Iraq War, and was now in a vegetative state, living in a Tehran rest home. The second had become the Iranian ambassador to Kuwait, so it wouldn't be easy to reach him. The third had renounced his past and become a dissident; he had been imprisoned for a few articles he'd written that were critical of the regime. The fourth had been elected to Parliament, where he constantly fell asleep during the sessions and had no clout. The only man left had for a long time been the undersecretary to the minister of the interior. He was our best bet.

I called his office to make an appointment, but the secretary very courteously told me that she herself could help me with any problem I might have. To get past her, I had to use Ali's name: "He told me," I said, "that I have to deliver his message myself." I was given an appointment for the next day.

Undersecretary Akbar had the customary beard, a bald spot at the top of his head, and slippers on his feet. Over his wide, gray pants, he wore a blue-checkered shirt, with a buttoned-up collar. Between his fingers he held a *tasbih*, a string of prayer beads; an agate ring sparkled on his finger. He seemed the very picture of an executive, a man responsible for administering the will of the state. Akbar's appearance was a living testimony to the values he believed in—or at least what he wanted to believe in.

He glanced very briefly at my face the moment I entered the room. This was part of the normal routine. The fundamentalists avoided looking at women in the face, because they have been told that, according to certain scriptures, men and women should never look at each other's faces, let alone make eye contact. That wasn't all. To be admitted into the office I had to wear a black chador. It was impossible to enter any public office without one. And all women, whether Iranian or foreign, Muslim or non-Muslim, had to wear a *manteau*, a kind of overcoat, and a foulard. If you break any of these laws you are considered to have committed a crime and can be certain that you'll be punished.

Akbar rose from his desk and accompanied me to the sitting area reserved for guests. An assistant immediately brought us tea and pastries. After settling into the chair in front of me, Akbar constantly shifted his eyes, staring at every object in the room and finally at the ground. I had a lot of trouble focusing on what I was supposed to say. But I laid out the problem, trying not to sound aggrieved. I told him that the apartment belonging to Alì and Parì was their single inheritance from their parents, that it was only unoccupied temporarily and soon the owners would return. I frequently mentioned Alì, bringing up his medals, loyalty, and heroism; obviously I didn't mention Javad, or Abbas.

Akbar nodded vacantly, his gaze still moving in every direction. After about ten minutes he interrupted me in a rather rude manner, and said that he knew Alì very well. They'd gone to elementary school together and they'd been friends ever since. And he had always known Simin, Hossein, Parì, and—here he allowed a significant pause—the others. He knew all there was to know; he knew *everything*, he said, underscoring the word. I felt like a schoolgirl who was about to be punished.

Gradually, as he spoke, I began to recall exactly who he was. His father had a butcher's shop; Akbar had been a very timid child and once, I remembered, I'd even helped him with an essay for school.

Telling him of those childhood memories seemed to have unblocked something within him, because now he became more relaxed and inclined to help me. As we sipped our tea, he said that he would be able to postpone Parì's eviction for a few months, but it was necessary to find a permanent legal solution as soon as possible.

"That's why I'm here," I said.

He seemed absorbed by his *tasbih*. Finally he explained what was usually done in "these cases," as he put it, emphasizing both words.

Parì had to transfer her property into the possession of someone she trusted, who then had to move into the apartment. After this, she had to draw up a separate contract, in which the new inhabitant was to acknowledge that Parì was the true owner. That would give Parì the right to reclaim the property as soon as she returned to Tehran. This was the only option. What it effectively meant was that the tenant would have use of the home, but Parì would maintain ownership.

I couldn't believe it—here I was, a lawyer, and I hadn't figured it out myself, while a man who spent all day caressing his *tasbih* had.

Seeing how perplexed I was, Akbar said, "Every law has its unwritten clauses."

"I know."

"So you know that those unwritten clauses tell you how to bypass the law."

I wanted to object, but I nodded, conceding the argument.

"Find a person of faith to whom she can entrust the apartment," he said. "I'll find a way to delay the property seizure for another six months. I can't do more than that."

I thanked him and stood to leave. Before exiting the room, as the assistant cleared away the tea and Akbar returned to his desk, I remembered a conversation I had with Parì before leaving London, in which she explained to me why she couldn't return to Iran. Many university professors like her had ended up on the list of citizens who were forbidden to travel abroad. Most of the time they weren't even notified of this: until the one day when they arrived at the airport and, when they handed over their passport, the agents told them that they couldn't leave the country.

I asked Akbar: "Can Parì return to Iran?"

For the second time the undersecretary was forced to look at my face. "Everyone can return to Iran."

"I'm sorry. What I meant to say was, if she returns to Iran, will she be able leave the country again?"

From Akbar's irritated expression I could tell that he was already regretting having agreed to help me. He didn't say anything, but turned to his computer, and for a few minutes I stood there, in front of his desk, waiting for a response. At last he said, "There's not any problem. Parì isn't on the list."

I gave a sigh of relief—finally some good news. I said goodbye again to Akbar, with a gesture of sincere gratitude, and hurried out.

Parì sent me a proxy letter from London and I went to work. I contacted the elderly cousin that we had chosen to take possession of her property and the two of us signed all of the necessary documents—the one intended for the authorities and the private one, for the two of them, that declared the apartment, and everything in it, belonged to Parì and that the cousin had no other property rights.

That evening, on the telephone, Parì thanked me profusely. She was even more enthusiastic when I told her that she wasn't on the feared list. Immediately I began to talk about her return: she should take a monthlong holiday and come back for *Nowruz*, the Persian New Year, so we could spend a few days together and she could see all her old friends again. Her voice became more lively as she started to imagine elaborate plans to see everyone.

A few weeks later I was contacted by Akbar's secretary, at his request. I was surprised and alarmed: What did this mean? Were there complications? A reversal now would be heartbreaking, especially after our brief euphoria. We scheduled a meeting for the following week. I was filled with anxiety in the interim, and when the moment arrived it was almost a relief to put on that odious black chador in preparation for the appointment. When I entered his office, Akbar told me he'd learned, happily, that the apartment had been taken care of.

"Now that we've resolved Parì's problem, it's time to deal with Alì's," he added, as if that could also be resolved with a proxy contract.

I looked at him uncomprehendingly. I knew that Alì had left Iran and lived in Lyon, but no one had told me about his problems, not even Parì.

"For a man like Alì, who loved Imam Khomeini so profoundly, and who fought with valor for his nation, it's a great shame that he should live in France. Ms. Ebadi, you and Parì should convince him to return to Iran."

"Alì is an adult, in full control of his mental faculties," I replied. "Far be it for me to tell him where he should live."

Akbar played with his *tasbih*. "Alì's problem is that the counterrevolutionaries have misled him. Once he returned to Tehran he lost his revolutionary spirit. He kept going on about how, after Khomeini's death, the Islamic Republic went off on the wrong path. But our efforts to bring him back to reality had no effect."

I couldn't stop myself from interrupting him. "Don't you think that, at the beginning of the Revolution, everyone was more pious than they are now?"

Akbar was visibly irritated by my cutting tone. Yet he tried not to give in to his anger, and to respond calmly.

"Of course," he said. "The figure of the Imam had immense value for all of us. But he was in fact a man and, sooner or later, he had to leave us. Ayatollah Khamenei is doing his best for Iran, and for Islam. Just because a handful of officials are corrupt doesn't mean that we have to be skeptical of the entire system. Alì lost faith in the fundamental principles of the regime."

"Did you ever ask Alì why he had allowed himself to be misled, as you say, by the counterrevolutionaries?"

Akbar looked at me as if he were sincerely hurt by my hostility. This was now the third time. I might have been pulling the cords too tight, but his self-satisfied manner had infuriated me.

"I believe that Alì lost his faith," he said. "He questioned everything and finally he left for France. He applied for refugee status, defaming himself and all of us. I ask you to convince him to return. Tell him that we'll be waiting with open arms."

I felt as if I'd been punched in the stomach. It was the fear that something terrible was going to happen—yet another grim surprise.

"And if I don't want to? If I don't try to convince Alì to return? Will Parì's apartment again be in danger?"

"No, Ms. Ebadi. Your friend won't lose her apartment, she has every right to continue to be its owner. What we're talking about is Alì returning to Iran. And how, if he does, everything will be forgiven."

I was extremely disturbed when I left the meeting. Akbar's attitude had been serene, his tone magnanimous, and he made no threats, but nevertheless I felt an ominous cloud hovering over me. I had long ago learned to trust my instincts. Sure, it was silly of me to ask about Parì's apartment—that wasn't the point. And Alì's soul, or his mental condition, aren't really what interested

Akbar. They wanted Alì to return to the ministry because, as a former commanding officer in the military and ministerial functionary, they worried he might pass intelligence secrets to the Westerners. He had seen too much, and his eyes and mouth needed to be shut. So his "loss of faith" would be "pardoned." But what would happen after that?

That night I called Parì and told her everything. I asked her to keep me informed, so that if Akbar wanted to see me again, I'd know what to tell him. As to the possibility that Alì would change his mind and decide to return to Iran, she was very skeptical: "That'll never happen. If I were him I'd never come back. But I'll let you know what he says."

She called me a few weeks later to confirm that Alì had no intention ever to step inside Iran again, at least not while it was still an Islamic Republic. He had entered a French governmental program for the protection of political refugees, with the hope to prevent the Iranian secret services from finding him. He said that he couldn't give Parì his telephone number or his address, because that would be dangerous for both of them, if they did try to torture her to get information. But he promised, every once in a while, he'd let her know that he was still alive.

26

Return to Tehran

On *Nowruz*, the Persian New Year that falls on the spring equinox, Iranian families celebrate the passage of time by honoring ancient customs. You set a table with a copy of the Koran, a few traditional plates, and various other objects. At least seven of these objects must have a name that begins with the letter that, in Farsi, is called *Sin*. These objects usually include: a vase of *sonbol*, hyacinths; a bowl of *senjed*, the dried fruit of a silverberry tree, and one of *somaq*, dried sumac ground into a powder; *serkeh*, vinegar; *sib*, apple; *sir*, garlic; *sekkeh*, gold coins; *sabzeh*, the herb that sprouts from certain grains or lentils; and *samanù*, a cereal paste.

The table, which is called *Haft Sin*, sits untouched for the full duration of *Nowruz*. With the exception of the Koran, which represents the holiday's religious aspect, the objects symbolize the blessings of nature, bounty, and beauty. At the moment when the old year gives way to the new, all the members of the family gather around the *Haft Sin* to exchange good wishes and share presents with the youngest children. Then you visit relatives and friends, and the children visit the most elderly family members at their *Haft Sin*, where more blessings and gifts are exchanged.

All over the world, wherever there's a community of Iranians, no matter how small, *Nowruz* is celebrated. In Iran, office workers are given six days off, while schools and universities have a two-week break, to ensure that there's enough time to visit friends and relatives. Those vacation days usually become exhausting rounds of seeing many people.

In those last relatively calm years before the deaths of Abbas and Javad, Simin had taken to celebrating the third day of *Nowruz* with a huge party at her house that quickly became a required stop for all of her friends and relatives. It was mandatory not just because she was an elderly woman and highly respected in the community but because it was a great joy to sit at her table. She always spent at least a week preparing all of her special dishes.

The ritual began with her and Parì going shopping: the two women visited all of their trusted stores and ordered lamb of the highest quality, chickens from the countryside, the whitest, finest rice, raisins, large grapes, almonds, and crunchy pistachios, and many pounds of tomatoes, celery, eggplants, fava beans, and peas. The shop owners had known Simin for years and they looked forward to her visit—not only because of the size of her order, but because it was confirmation that for another year their store was deemed, by a woman with such discriminating taste, as one of the best markets in Tehran. She wouldn't hesitate to send back an entire crate if a single handful of lentils didn't reach her high standards.

There followed intense preparations, during which both Simin and Parì cut down as much as possible on any activities that might keep them away from the kitchen. She had established a precise schedule that covered every phase. from marinating the meat to cooking the rice, every step had its rules, and you had to follow them. I still remember the intense scent of mint and lemon that would fill the house in those days and wafted from the clothes and bodies of the mother and daughter, trailing them like a wake as they walked down the street.

Parì would even ask for time off from work so she could help her mother full-time. When finally *Nowruz* arrived they were both tired and tense from their long hours together in the kitchen and the constant battles over the proper amounts of coriander or poppy seeds. With every new course that appeared on the table, you could read the anxiety on their faces before their guests took the first bites, Simin worrying that it wouldn't live up to her legacy, Parì terrified that her mother would hold her responsible for a dish's shortcomings because she'd been careless with the saffron. As tolerant as Simin could be when it came to her children's various indiscretions, she was equally unforgiving in her domain—the kitchen.

After Abbas's death, Simin gave up celebrating *Nowruz,* using her heart attack as an excuse, and the large reunions at her home became a distant memory. For more than fifteen years the apartment remained closed to friends and relatives. In the meantime some of them died, some moved, and others left the country. But every one of them who still lived in Tehran would be invited to a large lunch that Parì planned as commemoration for her mother and her family. As she'd promised, she entered Iran shortly before the new year. Fortunately her return avoided any conflict, and there were no problems with the authorities. Following Simin's example, she ordered enough food for a feast and spent almost a week cleaning, reorganizing the apartment, cooking, and reorganizing again. She invited her guests to arrive on the third day of the holiday in keeping with the tradition, but she wouldn't see anyone before then.

I went to the reunion with my mother. As soon as we entered we could see that nothing had changed. The apartment was the same, the furniture, too. The kitchen table had been pushed next to the living room table and this took up half the room. On the embroidered tablecloth there sparkled colored candles, bought specially for the occasion, one for each guest. I found mine; as always, it was yellow.

Photographs of Hossein and Simin hung on the wall in silver frames. Right beneath them were smaller portraits of Abbas and Javad. Their candles were lit on a small table, as if they were still alive.

Parì greeted us warmly. She gave my mother a long hug and whispered a few words into her ear; my mother caressed Parì's back with the same affectionate gesture that she used with her grandchildren. My friend smiled and her lips trembled, but she soon got hold of herself, resuming her role as the perfect host. She wouldn't disappoint Simin.

All during the party she went back and forth tirelessly between the living room and the kitchen, greeting everyone, saying a few words here and there and moving on without waiting for a response. She refused to let anyone help her, honoring her mother's motto that guests are guests and shouldn't be made to work. When someone told her that her *chelow kebab* was just as good as her mother's, her eyes sparkled with happiness. She leaned close to me and whispered, "Everything's in its right place, just as if *maman* was here with us. She always told me, 'Parì, I don't want the door to my home to be shut after my death. I beg you, I don't want to be forgotten.' If you hadn't saved the apartment, I couldn't have done any of this. Thank you." Then she ran off to get the next course.

After the meal, which indeed had been up to Simin's standards, Parì gave a brief speech in honor of her mother. Her voice betrayed her profound emotions, and we all discretely reached for our handkerchiefs to wipe away our tears. Parì promised that, as long as she lived, she would return to Tehran for *Nowruz* every year and hold this party. "I hope that doesn't upset you too much," she added, turning toward an aunt who was sobbing uncontrollably. We all burst into laughter and were again ready to celebrate the new year.

As we were saying our good-byes, Parì asked to see me the next day.

"In your office," she specified.

We agreed upon a time, and I was left to wonder what legal issues she might possibly have.

WHEN PARÌ CAME TO SEE ME she was joined by an elegant woman whom I'd never met before. The woman brought a splendid basket of roses and fragrant red carnations, which she gave me with a smile that was kind and confident at the same time. She seemed like an important guest: a determined, forceful person; I liked her directness, but she also made me feel slightly uneasy.

"Congratulations on the prize," she said, immediately taking charge of the conversation. She was referring to the Nobel Peace Prize, which I'd just been awarded. "I hope you'll accept these flowers." I thanked her and asked them to sit down. Parì was standing to one side, and hadn't said a word—in the daylight she seemed changed from the previous night, when she'd made every effort to present herself as Simin's perfect daughter. Now she seemed a woman of the West, with her plucked eyebrows, neatly manicured fingernails, and a certain formalness in conducting what was apparently going to be a business meeting—though I soon found it didn't have anything to do with money.

It had to do with bodies.

The woman with Parì introduced herself as Behnaz. "I come to you as a representative of the families whose relatives are in Khavaran," she said. "I'd like to make a request. I hope you might be able to help us."

I smiled, encouraging her to continue. As she spoke, I sipped my tea. The intensity of her expression unnerved me, and I felt the need to keep my hands occupied.

"We'd like permission to construct, at our expense, a monument for the dead. We've already made a formal request to the authorities, but no one has bothered to give us any response." Behnaz's eyes were fixed on mine.

Khavaran was conceived as a cemetery for non-Muslims and originally accepted deceased adherents of the Baha'i religion, Hindus, and Christians. Later it became the regime's great mass grave; they eliminated any dissidents they considered atheists or nonbelievers—members of the Tudeh, primarily. The Muslim dissidents, such as the mojahedin, were buried in the new cemetery of Behesht-e Zahra. Obviously the same authority figures who had ordered those people's deaths—and who were reluctant even to allow them proper burials—would never allow such a monument to be erected at a mass grave. This seemed self-evident to me.

Parì saw my perplexity and jumped in. "Given your work and the fact that, with this award, you've become an international figure, we thought that you might be able to help us by speaking out for our cause."

There was a long silence, during which a number of thoughts rushed through my mind. I told myself that it was a good cause, but a lost cause. I felt, as a lawyer, that I should tell my client this, but I wondered how best to convey myself. And above all, I wondered why Parì had allowed herself to become involved with this. Then I thought of Javad, his impudent smile and dark, luminous eyes, and of Abbas, the victim of an equal, but different, injustice. And I understood that Parì hadn't changed. I had been wrong to mistake her for a Western woman who had turned her back on Iran. In reality, she'd taken her grief and her nostalgia with her; it was only that in London she couldn't give voice to all of those feelings. Here, in Tehran, the past had returned with all its power; she had the same sad, proud look in her eyes as Behnaz. The only difference was that Behnaz was an older woman, having remained in Iran and seen more sons die every day, until she had nothing left to lose. Parì, on the other hand, risked losing her country forever, so soon after finally being able to return to it. I also realized, in that moment, why my friend had chosen *Nowruz* for her visit. Certainly it was in honor of her mother, but also because the families of the dead left in Khavaran met twice a year to commemorate their loved ones: once in the last week of the month of *Shahrivar*, August 14th through the 21st, and again in the last week of the month of *Esfand*, March 14th through the 21st right before *Nowruz*. Parì had clearly participated in that meeting.

My long silence had become awkward and I saw the shoulders of my visitors lower almost imperceptibly, as if in anticipation of a refusal. I said simply, "I don't have a good relationship with the authorities. You know that."

Behnaz shook her head and closed her eyes. "I had hoped that you, of all people, after having won the Nobel, would be able to help us. Your involvement would surely be given more weight than ours. I realize now, however, that our cause doesn't interest you. I'm sorry to have wasted your time."

She had misunderstood my hesitation.

"No, it's not that. I simply want you to know in advance that it's a lost cause. I will accept it, and I'll do everything I can, but I don't expect us to gain anything, and you shouldn't either. . . . I'm with you." Without wanting to be more explicit in front of a woman I didn't know, I gave a pointed look to Parì. Did she realize, I wondered, that the price she'd be paying was the possibility of permanent exile? I saw her nod lightly, an infinite sadness in her eyes. Meanwhile Behnaz, relieved, smiled and nodded.

"We don't expect to win," she said. "We just want our voices to be heard. That would be enough—for us and for the memory of those we've lost." As she said this she stood up and extended her hand.

We agreed on the next steps we would take and said our good-byes. I stayed alone in my office, arranging the large basket of roses and carnations, wondering where all of this would lead.

Iranian flowers, in fact all Middle Eastern flowers, have a splendor that I've never found elsewhere. In the West flowers are an ornament, often a very beautiful one, but in the Islamic culture they're something more, perhaps due to the important role that Persian gardens have had for the last fifteen hundred years or more: a kind of *speculum mundi*, a microcosm meant to represent the variety of living beings. Or perhaps it's because the Koran proscribes a certain value to vegetation as a metaphor for eternal life. But seeing that the authorities didn't allow the planting of flowers to be used as a memorial to the dead in Khavaran, it seemed right to honor them with something else: a monument. Even though it would probably have to be a monument of words.

*   *   *

THAT AFTERNOON PARÌ CALLED to thank me. But I could sense the tension in her voice. Something was still wrong.

"So, Parì *joon*, what's going on?" I asked her casually.

"I'm a chicken," she confessed. "I was completely determined to come back here, but now I tremble about every little thing that happens." She paused a second before blurting out: "I'm afraid they're going to stop me at the airport. I leave in two days."

She was no longer the perfect hostess, nor was there any sign of the coolness that she'd shown in my office just a few hours earlier.

"What happens if they arrest me?" she asked. "If they're anxious to catch Alì, maybe they'll stop me and throw me in prison. They could torture me." I understood where this was coming from—I was well aware that her visits to Javad had left an indelible mark on her. I'd gone through the experience of prison myself, and I told her I'd do whatever I could to save her from the same fate. But even as I reassured her, my words sounded empty to my own ears: her fears were reasonable. We decided to see each other that night to figure out a good strategy. I didn't feel I could manage this all alone, so I asked my husband to join us—three minds being better than two.

We picked up Parì and drove north of Tehran to a small town that once was filled with summer homes built for the city's middle class, and was now considered a suburb. There was a quiet restaurant where we often went to escape from our routine and from the oppressive climate of the capital. Tehran is a beautiful city, with gorgeous views of the mountains, but in living there one has to endure a number of inconveniences. The worst of them, due to a population of more than twelve million, is the traffic. Second is the terrible pollution. The air in Tehran is so dirty that about sixty days a year the government releases advisories cautioning children and the elderly to stay inside their homes.

Nowruz is the best time to visit because many people leave the city for the holidays and schools and offices are closed, too. The nicest parts of Tehran can then finally come out of hiding—it's as if the rest of the year they're afraid of being covered by a blanket of people and pollution.

At dinner, we discussed Parì's concern that she might be arrested at the airport. I told her that she shouldn't worry; that kind of thing doesn't happen so much anymore, the international organizations were watching for all of the regime's tricks. But my husband, who was more realistic than me, had an idea. He reached into his pocket and pulled out his cellular phone. He put it on the table and pointed at it.

"Take it," he told Parì.

Parì laughed. "I don't understand. Are you giving me a present?"

This was his plan: since a cell phone could pick up voices even if it laid tucked inside a handbag, Parì could take it with her to the airport, and call us as soon as she got close to the passport control. She would then leave the phone on and place it back in her bag, so that we could listen. If something happened, we'd know right away and take immediate action.

Parì smiled. The idea seemed perfect. She only worried about the cell phone. "How can I get it back to you?"

My husband had a solution for that, too. His brother, who lived not far from London, would be flying back to Iran a week later. Once she arrived safely in England, Parì could get in touch with him and give him the phone.

For the rest of dinner she kept telling me what a clever man I'd married. And a generous one, too: though he pretended it didn't matter, a week without his cell phone was no small thing to him. Parì and I looked at him admiringly and were soon in good spirits again. Only then did we allow ourselves to gossip and talk about old memories, which my husband endured with the patience of a philosopher.

The day of her departure, my husband took Parì to the airport and I stayed at home, waiting for news. If something happened, we'd have to intervene as soon as possible so we wouldn't lose track of her. When the telephone rang I picked up immediately. Parì told me that she was about to go through passport control. Then she rested the cell phone in her bag and I waited, listening.

The clock in my kitchen marked the seconds. We'd had it for ten years and until that moment I'd never realized how sharp the noise of the second hand was. My forehead was beaded with sweat. Though the sounds were muffled, I could hear Parì giving her passport to the official. I tried to imagine the man. It wasn't difficult. He was most likely wearing a shirt buttoned up to his collar, and had a long beard.

There was a lengthy, silent pause, then the clicking of computer keys. I imagined Parì, like me, holding her breath. The man seemed to be taking longer than necessary. Sitting there in my kitchen I squeezed the telephone with my hand, the adrenaline rushing through my veins. I felt lost, powerless.

The man stopped typing. Silence.

"Here's your passport, sister."

Another silence. Then the rustling sound of the cell phone jostling in the bottom of the handbag. The noise of sliding doors, hurried footsteps, more sliding doors.

She called me again an hour later, from the shuttle that was taking her to the airplane.

I waited, listening, until Parì boarded the plane, and the connection broke off.

Six hours later the points of Jack's mustache peeked out from the crowd awaiting arriving flights at Heathrow, and he brought her home safely.

27

A Monument of Sand

I WAITED FOR PARÌ to call as soon as she arrived in London to reassure me that everything went all right, but there was no call, not from her or Jack. After two days, I finally phoned her house. No one picked up. Suddenly I was alarmed: perhaps our trick had been discovered and they'd arrested her at the airport. That would mean that Parì was in a prison somewhere in Iran. I started to bombard her voice mail with messages, in the hope that she'd respond. Meanwhile my fears grew and I couldn't sleep. If only I'd figured out sooner that she'd been abducted, I could've intervened before they executed her, but now I had no idea where she might be or how to find her. I thought about contacting various international organizations, but decided to wait until I'd at least heard from Jack. If Parì hadn't returned, surely he would have told me so. The confusion was exasperating, as was the feeling that there was nothing I could do.

After a week, I finally received a telephone call from London. It was Jack. He assured me that Parì had arrived safely and he apologized for their delay in telling me so. He was terse and seemed purposely evasive. She wasn't able to talk to me right then, that she'd call as soon as possible, he said. I wanted to know more, but I couldn't speak English very well to explain it to him. So I tried to put my heart at rest, hoping that my friend would contact me soon.

In the meantime I started working on the monument to those buried at Khavaran. I decided that the first step was to call the mayor's office and ask for a meeting. I knew that it'd be difficult to pursue through the official channels, but I wanted to try every avenue for Behnaz and Parì.

I sipped some hot tea, took a deep breath, and picked up the phone. I gave the secretary my basic information and said that I would like to meet with the mayor. On the other end of the line there was a moment of stunned silence. Then the secretary responded that she first had to understand exactly what my question was; if it contributed to the common good, she would connect me to the appropriate department. In any case, she said, the mayor was not available to see me.

I briefly stated my business, and the secretary paused again, this time for longer. Finally she said, "You should address your request to the Department of City Planning. If it corresponds with their land use regulations, it may be accepted."

I doubt it, I thought, but I didn't say anything.

I immediately delivered a letter to the Department of City Planning. I was told that I'd receive a reply within three days. But when I went in person three days later they had no response. I was bothered: what kind of men were these, hiding behind bureaucracies and even lacking the courage to reject a request? I would have preferred a clear, explicit denial, but instead I was met with silence.

THEN I SENT A FORMAL WRITTEN REQUEST to the Parliament. After a month without a response I resigned myself to the likelihood that they'd never respond. I had no way of knowing whether anyone had even received my letter.

Next I went to the Ministry of the Interior, where an employee told me what I already knew, which is that the issue pertained to the Department of City Planning and that I should inquire there. So I went back to that office again, presenting them with the same letter I had submitted a month earlier. Someone assured me that I'd have a response in two days.

I returned punctually two days later. They told me that my request was still being processed by the city council and that I needed to wait three more days for their response. It never came.

"What did you expect?" My husband asked me. "Did you think they were going to build a monument for all the people they'd shot?" Of course he was right. I'd always known that this was going to be impossible. But no one, including my husband, could appreciate that the complete absence of a response for those people lost in a mass grave was much, much worse than receiving a negative one. I wanted to express my anger somehow, to denounce them for their cowardly silence.

At the time, the mayor of Tehran was a man named Mahmoud Ahmadinejad.

The reformists had lost the 2003 elections because Khatami's moderate government failed to fulfill the expectations of the Iranian people: the plans they had proposed during their last campaign had not been realized. The people, tired of broken promises, boycotted the general elections, refusing to go to the polls. The fundamentalists, who usually constituted about 15 percent of the electorate, were left with no opposition, so they triumphed. Ahmadinejad was elected mayor of Tehran and two years later he became the president of the Islamic Republic of Iran.

It was under his presidency that the issue of a nuclear Iran became one of the most controversial problems in the Middle East, and risked giving the United States a reason to invade Iran and assume control of the oil industry. Ahmadinejad looked for any excuse to start a conflict with the West; for example, one of the first things he said after his presidential inauguration was that the State of Israel must be "wiped off the face of the earth."

As Tehran's mayor a man like him would never agree to meet me. It was also clear that Javad and all the other people whose remains were in the desert of Khavaran would not have their legacies marked with the permanency of a monument; their tomb would only have the anonymous windswept sand dunes.

That day I admitted my defeat. Not even the Nobel Peace Prize was enough.

I summoned my courage and called Parì. Jack picked up and said she couldn't come to the phone. I insisted, saying that it was urgent. That's when Jack revealed to me the mystery behind Parì's silence.

28

The Paris Sky

ALÌ WAS ADJUSTING to his new life, even though it felt incomplete—he lived like a fugitive, and felt constantly on edge. He had studied French for long enough to gain admittance to a law school, and moved to Paris. He attended classes, but communicated with the other students as little as possible: it was too exhausting to keep track of all the lies he was forced to tell to maintain his false identity. Ironically, all of the different personas that the witness protection program had asked him to assume had a lot in common with his true self: they were all sad, reserved, and solitary.

He rented a room in a pension near the Père Lachaise Cemetery, run by an old woman who trusted what she saw in his eyes and felt sorry for him. He was too close to the graveyard, and every morning he was awakened by the heavy, prolonged chiming of the bells.

"I met an old school friend of yours," he told Parì, in one of their Sunday phone conversations. "Once in a while I'm able to talk with someone."

He could hear his sister, on the other end of the line in London, stiffening and holding her breath. The news didn't please her. "Do you trust him?" she asked.

"Like I trust my own eyes," he said confidently.

Alì had run into him one day in the Place de la Bastille—or

more precisely on a small side street, lined with restaurants, where he'd decided to splurge on a nice lunch. He'd spotted his friend, and waved to get his attention. "Siamak!" he'd called out, with unrestrained joy. Siamak turned abruptly and looked around, scanning the people passing by. Finally, after a momentary hesitation, he recognized Alì and invited him to his table, where he was drinking an orange juice. Looking out into the crowded street, he whispered, "I don't go by Siamak anymore. Then again, I've changed names so many times that I don't even remember what I'm supposed to call myself now."

He had lived for a year and a half in Spain, where he worked as a waiter in a popular restaurant, and for the past five months he'd been in Paris under a new identity. Alì felt relieved; seeing an old friend who, like him, was living as a fugitive. He felt he could become himself again. Siamak, or whatever he was called now, talked to Alì with the same frankness as always, which had a calming effect on him. For an hour they spoke nonstop.

"Let's stay in touch—perhaps we can see each other once in a while," Siamak had suggested.

Alì wasn't sure this was a good idea; the only people he saw with regularity were his university professors, to whom he was nothing more than a brown face in the crowd of students, and the woman who ran the pension, who was nearly blind. But he set a meeting with his friend for the following week; he proposed meeting in the street, so he didn't have to give him any address. Siamak said OK, adding that he never gave out his own address either, and he didn't have a telephone number.

They continued to see each other like this for a couple of months. Once a week, always on a different day, they met in different places, and then wandered through the city. And always in a different neighborhood. Together they explored every corner of Paris, the tourist areas as well as the more hidden, unknown ones, while never calling each other by their names, fearful they might be overheard. Alì even avoided saying his friend's name while on the phone with Parì, out of fear that their call might be monitored and that he might implicate Siamak, or himself.

But he did tell Parì about their long walks together, the conversations about their distant—and now dead—former lives and, after some time had passed, he told her that his friend had been to his house. The taboo of keeping their addresses secret from each other had given way under the strength of the confidence they had developed between them; there was also the fact that their interminable walks through the city had lost their novelty and had begun to feel exhausting. So they often found themselves in Alì's apartment, playing chess or backgammon. These meetings became the highlight of Alì's life. The only time he felt alive.

About a week before my conversation with Jack, Siamak had gone to visit Alì at his pension, greeted the old woman who lived on the first floor of the building, walked up to the third floor, and knocked on the door, using the agreed-upon code. Alì opened the door right away. Soon they were chatting about their day, while playing backgammon and sipping tea.

"I'm happy to see you," Alì looked at his friend, a backgammon piece raised in his hand—breaking a rule of the game.

"C'mon," said Siamak impatiently, his eyes fixed on the piece. "Play."

But Alì put his hand over the board.

"No," he said, almost timidly. "I'm serious. When I talk with you, it feels like a weight is lifting from my soul. For a few hours I can really be myself again." Alì had never been so forthcoming, either as a boy or a man, and the last months of solitude certainly hadn't helped.

Perhaps Siamak was equally reticent, because his eyes now clouded over. He seemed embarrassed, even irritated, by Alì's sudden admission, or perhaps by the interruption in the game.

"We'd better just start all over again," muttered Siamak, grabbing the dice.

Alì, surprised and a little bit wounded by his friend's coldness, retreated inwardly. He straightened his shoulders and stood up.

"You're right," he said, nodding stiffly. "But first I'm going to make another pot of tea."

He was at the door to the kitchen when his friend called after him.

"Alì," said Siamak, in a conciliatory tone. It sounded like he was going to apologize for his callousness. Alì turned around, ready to forgive him.

Siamak fired two bullets into Alì's forehead.

Then he left the apartment, kicking the backgammon board onto the floor.

This was the first news that Parì had received upon returning from Tehran.

"Your brother left me your number, saying that I should call you in case of an emergency."

Parì didn't know who it was, she'd never heard this voice before, but in her mind's eye she immediately pictured a small old woman with a slow gait and a sympathetic face, just as Alì had described the proprietor of the pension. Anxious, the woman gave her a foggy, jumbled account of what had happened. A man that she had often seen visit arrived at around five in the afternoon, then she thought that the two of them left together. After not seeing Kaddour (which was the name that Alì had used with her) enter or leave for two days, she went up to his room on the third floor. In the middle of the hallway she saw some dark spots on the tiling, and didn't go any further. She had let the police open the door.

Parì thanked the woman and hung up, cutting off her confused explanations and apologies for the state of her health, heart, nerves. Parì had to go to Paris, identify her brother's body, and make arrangements for a funeral—another one. For a minute she stood frozen, staring at the telephone. This was the first time that, after hearing bad news, she didn't feel an immediate sense of grief. Instead she felt resignation. She thought no one could feel so resigned to death, unless she had died many times already.

A few days later the police put together the facts. Thanks to the identification given by the old woman at the pension, and some nearby shop owners who had seen the two men walk past them, side by side, they identified Siamak. He worked for the Iranian Embassy in Paris, and he'd left his post, and France, on the same day that he'd shot Alì. Even before she had departed from London, Parì knew the assassin wouldn't be apprehended. And in Paris—as she sat in an office with olive green walls, signing a pile of papers—she felt no rage, or vengeance. It was clear enough what had happened. It didn't matter if the killer paid for his sin: the true culprit, the Islamic Republic, would go unpunished.

When she left the building she was swallowed by a fog that covered the entire city. She squinted, and remembered when she told Alì the news of Javad's arrest.

"Lots of brave soldiers risk death every day on the front. Why should I worry about Javad any more than them?"

That's what he'd said. Parì had changed the subject immediately, unable to believe that Alì could talk about his brother that way—unable to believe that Alì was more loyal to Khomeini than to his own blood. She didn't see how his political views could overwhelm the stronger, more profound bonds of family.

It seemed ironic the way Alì's words could be used against him. These thoughts went through Parì's head, over and over, as she walked without any strength left in her body, beneath the gray Paris sky.

29
A Family Reunion

PARÌ SPENT SEVERAL months in a clinic after suffering a serious nervous breakdown that had weakened her body and spirit.

"No stress," was the doctor's advice. "And no news from Iran."

Jack, ever dutiful to his beloved, obeyed the doctor's orders. He shielded her from grief, from old memories, from suffering, from rage—and also from me. But I knew she'd recover—it was her nature.

Every day he visited her, and held her cold hands, thinking of all the times when they would lie together in bed and she'd ask him to warm up her hands. Now he did it every day, even though she didn't ask him anymore. In fact she didn't ask him anything anymore. Still, he tried each day to rekindle her love of life, and of him, chatting cheerfully—even incessantly—and bringing her small gifts of fruit and sweets, and brightly colored paintings that he'd made especially for her. He took her on walks through the park of the clinic—first in a wheelchair, then holding her under her arms, proceeding slowly, as if she was an old woman. Jack had gotten in the habit of writing down every funny thing that happened to him during his days, and he'd rattle off one after another in the hope of making her laugh. If he ran out of things to tell her, he started talking about the weather. The only thing he feared were her questions.

But she didn't have any. She listened, she drank tea, she let him lead her on walks. She participated listlessly in their conversations, often limiting herself to nodding along.

"It takes time," said the doctor. "A lot of time and a lot of patience," he added, glancing at the woman lying motionless in the hospital bed.

Jack had time and patience, those weren't the problems. But every day, just before he opened the door to her room, he was assailed by a sudden, irrational fear of finding an empty bed, discovering that she had given up, that his Parì finally couldn't take any more. He tried to shake off his fear and forced himself to turn the door handle. Jack was somewhat ashamed of himself for feeling that way, but still each time he couldn't help but breath a sigh of relief. Fortunately Parì was still there, alive—but always entirely disinterested in what was going on around her.

Parì told me all of this on the occasion of her second visit to Tehran for *Nowruz*. She had called several months earlier to apologize for her long silence and to invite me to the dinner that a year ago she promised she would host. Then she asked if she could see me beforehand, just the two of us. There was something she wanted to tell me.

We met in the café that we used to go to when we were younger, near the university. Parì was still thin, but not in the same healthy way as before, when she had been toned and energetic. This new weight loss had hollowed out her face; her eyes seemed enormous. Her bob was the same as always, her makeup and complexion, too, but her face was different. Not unattractive, but faded somehow. When she spoke about Alì, I understood exactly who she reminded me of: her mother in the later years, broken by strife and tragedy. Parì had the same fatigue in her voice, the same note of depression.

The doctor had urged her not to return to Tehran so soon. But she wouldn't listen to reason. She had promised to make the *Nowruz* dinner and she would keep her word. Jack joined her on the trip and helped her through it, making sure that she took her prescriptions and didn't have any new setbacks. He even did the cooking for her.

"Finally he does something, " joked Parì. "You see how much it pains me to see him in the kitchen?"

I burst into laughter, not because of the joke itself, but because I felt that she wanted me to laugh, to demonstrate to me—and to herself—that she was back. I understood that this impulse came from her head and not her heart, but I was somewhat reassured nonetheless. I knew that I could count on Parì's willpower and her stubbornness.

On the day of the dinner, I arrived at her house very early so that I could help her in the kitchen. She repeated, annoyed, her mother's mantra that guests were guests and shouldn't be put to work, and she tried to get me to sit on the couch. Finally I convinced her at least to let me chop the vegetables.

"Only that, nothing else," she mumbled, in a playful tone. "Otherwise who knows what kind of mess you'll make." Then she said to Jack: "I beg you, please don't put any dried fruit into my *chelow kebab*. He still hasn't learned how to do it."

We kept joking the rest of the afternoon. Jack smiled while he washed the greens, happy to see Parì in such high spirits. Despite the doctor's orders, Parì was determined to hold another *Nowruz* feast in grand style and she pursued her goal with all the energy she could muster, but when the door opened to the first guests it was clear that the evening wouldn't have the same atmosphere as the previous year. Her friends and relatives had recently found out about Ali's death and the thought of yet another wrenching loss hung over us like a shadow. During dinner everyone tried to keep the conversation going, but it felt forced. For the first time that I could remember, the most silent person in the room was Parì, who was still dressed in her mourning clothes and sat in Simin's old place, watching us with an absent look on her face. With the nervous compliments and vague mutterings, the dinner soon became exhausting, and finally there was no sound other than the monotonous clinking of the cutlery.

It was Parì who broke the silence. "I want to thank you all for coming this year, especially after yet another misfortune has struck my family. Struck me, I should say, because there's no one else left." Here her voice trembled and we could see in her face the effort she was making to hold back the tears. "I think everyone's heard about Ali, but perhaps you don't know the details. You should at least know his true assassin: the Islamic Republic."

Then she told the story of his death. Her voice became tender and soft as she filled the absence that we had all sensed in the room. Her eyes were clear but steady as she turned to look at each of us, making sure to convey, to our minds and hearts, her grief and her rage.

"I'm sorry if, on this holiday, I've upset you. But this will be the last time. There is nothing left in Iran for me."

An old aunt rose suddenly to hug her, then all the guests, one by one, followed suit. With each embrace Parì seemed to regain a little more energy and found, in some hidden place within her, the source of the profound connection she felt to her land and her people—despite everything.

Everybody left soon after that. They all had the same gentle, tearful expression on their faces. I stayed behind to make sure that my friend was all right. I offered to help her clean up.

I was facing the wall where the family portraits hung. Hossein and Simin were above; the sons underneath. Now Alì had joined them, smiling on the day of his wedding.

"The wall is full. Let's hope no one else dies: I wouldn't know where to put another photo," said Parì quietly. And she started laughing, while two large tears fell down her cheeks. "I'd like to believe that they didn't die for nothing."

I hugged her, crying with her. "Alì was the baby," I heard her whisper, so quietly that I wasn't certain she had spoken. "My little baby."

Then she pulled back. Wiping away her tears she asked me about Khavaran.

"So, Miss Lawyer, I've noticed that there's still no monument. What happened?"

I quickly told her about the last few months that had made me and Behnaz give up our efforts.

"Forget it. Like a monument would've made up for the injustices. It's impossible to atone for such a thing."

Those words gave me a start—I remembered a famous statement made by the sociologist Alì Shariati, one of Islam's leading intellectuals, who died in Iran under mysterious circumstances a year before the Islamic Revolution. He had said, "If you can't eliminate injustice, at least tell everyone about it."

We couldn't build a monument to the memory of Javad and those who, like him, were victims of the regime. Nor could we honor the many families that had been broken, and destroyed by the political order that the Revolution, like a noxious wind, had swept over us. But we could at least tell everyone their stories, a tragedy that has been shared by an entire country. I proposed to Parì that I'd write all of it down. That way I could reveal everything that had happened. All she'd have to do was fax what I'd written to the United Nations.

Parì looked at me for a long time without speaking. Then she smiled.

"I'd be very happy if you did that. On one condition: you shouldn't limit your account to Javad. You should tell the stories of Abbas and Alì. They were victims of equal injustice. I would like the three of them to share the same destiny, even if it is only in the pages of a book."

31901050724741